RETIRE
INTENTIONALLY

STORIES AND STRATEGIES TO SPEND, GIVE, AND LIVE WITH CONFIDENCE

ZACHARY LARSON

RETIRE INTENTIONALLY

For More Information:
Fig Factor Media | figfactormedia.com

Layout by Fig Factor Media
Edited by Hilary L. Jastram

Printed in the United States of America

ISBN: 978-1-961600-15-7
Library of Congress Control Number: 2024919020

FIG
FACTOR
MEDIA

Dedication

To my clients who trusted me when I was young
and who've become friends as we've grown together.
I hope you've learned from me just as I've learned
from you.

Table of Contents

Get in Touch

www.intentgen.com

www.retire-intentionally.com

www.linkedin.com/in/zac-larson-intentional-generous

Foreword

In a world where the concept of retirement often conjures images of idle days and diminished purpose, *Retire Intentionally* offers a refreshing and transformative perspective. This book is not just a guide to financial freedom; it's a blueprint for living a life of meaning, fulfillment, and intentional impact in your later years.

I have known Zac for 16-plus years, and I can tell you from firsthand experience, he is the real deal. I have had the joy of knowing him as a friend, as a leader at a church where I served as pastor, as a strategist, as I helped him navigate the wonderful challenges of growing a business, and as someone who has benefitted from his wisdom on more than one occasion. I have the deepest respect and love for Zac and am filled with joy knowing that now, through this book, many more people will have the opportunity to learn from his wisdom.

Zac, a seasoned CERTIFIED FINANCIAL PLANNER™, has spent decades guiding individuals through the complex financial landscapes of their lives. But his approach goes far beyond the numbers. He understands that retirement is not merely an end to one's career but a new beginning. It is a chapter where time, wealth, and purpose intersect in powerful ways.

Through engaging stories and practical strategies, Zac empowers readers to transition from a mindset focused solely on net worth to one that embraces the profound possibilities of net income and net impact.

What sets this book apart is its deep understanding of the human experience in retirement. Zac doesn't just address the "how" of managing money; he delves into the "why" behind our financial choices, encouraging readers to align their resources with their values, passions, and the legacy they wish to leave behind.

Whether you are approaching retirement or already navigating its waters, this book will inspire you to live with intentionality, confidence, and joy.

Retire Intentionally is more than just a financial guide—it's a call to live your retirement years with the same purpose and vigor that defined your working life.

It is with great admiration and respect that I introduce this remarkable book, which I am confident will leave a lasting impact on all who read it.

With gratitude,
Glen Wagner
CEO/Founder, FinishStrong Group, LLC

Author's Note

"I'm going to Disney World!"

This iconic phrase, although cliché, has become a tradition for newly crowned champions (especially in the sporting world) to declare in celebration of their milestone achievement.

When my wife, Kristin, and I had four little boys (ages 3-8 at the time), we felt like we were champions as we moved them all through the potty-training phase, so we announced we would celebrate by going to Disney World!

Our trip was awesome, and I still have fond memories, but it wasn't always as magical as we had hoped. There were incredible experiences, thrilling adventures, great family time, relaxing moments, and lots of fun. But it was not stress-free, and it was not perfect. There were injuries, illnesses, meltdowns, and changes in plans. Although we had lots of free time, there were too many days in a row without routines, and that messed with everybody's mood. To top it off, it felt like money was disappearing before my eyes.

If you have successfully transitioned into retirement or are well-prepared for an upcoming retirement, you are also a champion! You have accomplished something many people will never achieve—the financial freedom to live without earning an income from your labors. So, champ... "Where are you going?" and "What's next?" You will, no doubt, hear those questions many times as people ask you about your retirement.

If done intentionally, this retirement phase can be filled with freedom, flexibility, fun, purpose, and incredible impact. Yet, without solid planning, it may not be as magical as you'd hoped. Most likely, it will not be stress-free, and it won't be perfect. There may be injuries or illnesses, plans will inevitably change, and questions will probably emerge about your purpose when you no longer have the routines and relationships of your professional life. And just like I did on our family trip, you may feel like money is disappearing right before your eyes.

From those perspectives, along with my experience of learning what people often go through that makes them feel unprepared or surprised at retirement, this book took shape...

During my professional career, I have worked with all types of people. Some have struggled or do struggle with finances, and they have a hard time making decisions to spend or give their money. I've partnered with others who confidently pursue their goals, intentionally shift finances toward their priorities, and quickly align actions with their aspirations.

I hope that by sharing some of my clients' stories and outlining key financial perspectives and processes, I can help you Retire Intentionally, so you can spend, give, and live with more confidence.

Before I go too far, too fast, into retirement strategies, it's important to clarify the concept of *retirement*, as it can mean many different things to different people. Retirement is a word filled with hope and opportunity for some and "good riddance" for others. For many, it means no more work, while for others, it means working in new and different ways.

Despite all its positive and negative connotations, most people associate retirement with an "ending." Through my work as a CERTIFIED FINANCIAL PLANNER™ (CFP®) during the last 20-plus years, I've partnered with people who have transitioned into and through retirement. While we have mostly focused on their finances, these clients (many of whom have become my friends) have taught me much about the emotional aspects of retirement.

My biggest and best realization is that, if done well (or *intentionally*), then retirement is less about an ending and more about a beginning. Retirement can be the beginning of a period where personal time, family time, travel time, and volunteer time take center stage. For the purposes of this book, I will share my perspectives on what I've learned, and I'll define retirement as a period that typically brings increased freedom in two areas:

- **Freedom with Finances**: You're in a phase where most, if not all, your expenses are covered by recurring income sources and withdrawals from investments instead of by paychecks from your work. Access to these savings and investments can cause anxiety and procrastination, or if planned thoughtfully, it can provide the flexibility to empower epic experiences and impact.
- **Freedom with Time**: Less time at "work" means more time for you to do whatever you want. My good friend, pastor/speaker/consultant Glen Wagner, of The FinishStrong Group, is quick to caution, though, as he regularly paraphrases Aristotle: "Time abhors a vacuum!" It's a reminder to all of us that if we don't fill our time intentionally, it will get filled with something…Retirement, at its best, allows you time to focus on yourself and your purpose and increase your impact on the people and places you care about.

That's how I think about retirement. The great part about this phase is that you get to define it for yourself.

I hope this book helps you more intentionally experience a chapter of life where you will likely have as much discretionary time as you did when you were a kid: Time to play, relax, or work at your own pace with the people you want, in the places you want.

With that in mind, I also want to pose a few questions and share some insights about what's in store for you in these pages:

First, and most importantly, ask yourself, what do you want to get out of this book? Are you trying to:

Grow your money?
Give your money?
Spend your money?
Save your money?

Whatever your priorities and goals are, I want you to be able to move toward them more articulately and intentionally.

Secondly, what will you do with the information or ideas you get as you read through this book?

I've often said, "Information without action is worthless."

I urge you not to just read or listen to the stories and strategies in this book but to follow the prompts at the end of each chapter and act, not just think!

My personal calling, and our company's mission,

is to empower people to live intentionally. That means I'm not telling you how to do things. You get to choose how to use the ideas and apply them to your life as you see fit. I will coach and encourage you to use your money intentionally, not accidentally!

A few additional thoughts before I dive in…

This Book Is Not:

- *A guide on how to accumulate the biggest net worth.* (It's more about how to use your net worth.)
- *A technical analysis.* (If you're looking for a graduate-level financial course, this is not it. However, if you want a storybook without any jargon, you'll also be disappointed. I will need to get into a few financial concepts and terms since they are critical to your retirement. Bear with me and try to learn them, as it will help you better focus on why you are doing what you are doing as you move through this process. These are anecdotes of what has worked for specific people, and they are examples of what might work for you.)
- *A manual detailing get-rich-quick schemes.* (I'm assuming that you're already rich or at least on the way; of course, rich is a relative term, and there's much more to come on that topic.)
- *The only right way to do things.* (There are many right ways, and I'll share a few.)

- *Designed to tell you what to do.* (You do you.)

This Book *Is* Focused On:

- *Retirement transitions.* (It's geared toward those planning to retire within the next 5-10 years and those who have retired within the last 5-10 years.)
- *Stories.* (I'm sharing stories of clients and non-clients who share at least one common trait—they're focused on living intentionally instead of accidentally. If you think they're doing it right, follow their lead. If it feels wrong to you, do it differently.)
- *Purpose.* (Money is obviously a big part of retirement conversations, but I'm more concerned about helping people do more with their money than I am about helping them *get* more money.)
- *Process.* (At IntentGen Financial Partners, we created a financial process to prepare and monitor retirement plans that empower people to live intentionally. I'll share parts of that process with you throughout this book, and anytime I reference "we" or "us," please know that I'm referring to my colleagues and company.)
- *Permission.* (This is an invitation for you to give yourself permission to do more... for yourself, your family, and others. It's an invitation to talk, think, and dream big...

with our company or those already in your corner... so you can live the intentional life you desire!)

This book is also a great tool for couples to use. You can read it with your spouse or partner to better understand definitions, the way specific assets and investments perform, when to switch from accumulation to distribution, and how to engage both of your accounts to best prepare you for your future together. As you continue to read, please keep in mind that I am addressing both individuals and couples.

There is a lot for us to cover together, so I've broken it down into three broad sections to simplify concepts:

- **Net Worth.** Admittedly, this section may feel the most basic to you, but its content is foundational. If you want to live an intentional retirement, you must come to grips with the fact that you and your retirement are not defined by your net worth. You won't live your life *because of* your net worth, but we need to get on the same page about what it is and how it impacts your retirement.
- **Net Income.** Your retirement life will be fueled *by* spending your net income. This consistent, tax-efficient, recurring income will provide you with the confidence to spend, give, and

live. It will provide peace of mind to keep spending when the markets are down and provide a paycheck so you can enjoy a normal life. Admittedly, this section will be the most technical, but I want to assure you that you don't need to become an expert at taxes and cash flow projections. Some core concepts are critical for you to learn, so you can gain more confidence to enjoy your money now—and later!

- **Net Impact.** Purpose. Passion. Experiences. Charity. Community. Events. Bucket lists. Volunteering. Coaching. Teaching. Chilling. This is what we've been waiting for… What do you want to do with your life, and how are your finances lined up to support and maximize your impact?

The stories and perspectives I'm sharing in the next sections span multiple decades of conversations and financial planning with people who are likely very similar to you. Clients' names and some characteristics have been changed to protect their identities. In stories where a spouse is referenced, please note that only one name of the couple may be used as this person has requested to be the primary contact. We encourage both spouses to be involved, as each person plays an equal role in the planning.

As you read about the decisions they've made, please keep in mind there is no room for judgment.

Like all of us, they are doing the best they can with what they have, according to their life experiences and priorities.

I hope their stories and my perspectives will inspire you to do the best you can with what *you* have. I'm confident that you will be able to do all of what you want to do more intentionally by the time we are done.

Net Worth

The Real Definition of Net Worth

"Happiness is the new rich. Inner Peace is the new success. Health is the new wealth. Kindness is the new cool."

~Syed Balkhi

My 13-year-old, Logan and I recently had a thought-provoking conversation after a song we were listening to referred to the singer's wealth as being *eight figures*! "Is that a million?" he asked. I encouraged him to re-work his math, and he quickly exclaimed, "Ten million—that's rich!"

"How much does it take to be rich?" I asked Logan that evening... I now ask you the same question: *How much does it take to be rich?*

Rich is a very relative term. The number you need for your retirement is a very relative term, as well. Years ago, a commercial for a financial firm referenced a number that people needed to retire. Of course, the number was different for everyone, but people walked around in this ad with their number in a bubble above their heads.

Imagine if there was a magic number you needed to greenlight your retirement.

How big would it be?
How would you calculate it?

Is that figure the peak of your wealth—a mountaintop number from which you'll descend the rest of your life?

Or is it a number that will grow with you as you age? And what happens to that number at the end of your life?

All these questions build upon themselves when we think about retirement as a number. There are even more questions to ponder when we think about wealth as a number.

My 13-year-old responded quickly when I asked him *how much it takes to be rich…* "I think it's actually more about how much you make," Logan said.

"So, how much?" I pressed. "Well…a hundred thousand dollars is a lot," he replied, "but that wouldn't make you rich. You could buy what you want, but you couldn't travel everywhere you want to go." He thought for a second and then emphatically concluded, "Probably a hundred and fifty thousand dollars… that would make you rich!" The mind of a 13-year-old… simple and profound all at once!

What do other sources say about how much income or wealth it takes to be rich? A quick online search highlights a *Yahoo! Finance* article from 2023 that notes if you have a net worth of $854,900, you are in the top 10% of the U.S. population.[1] Charles Schwab's "Modern Wealth Survey" from 2023 finds that 48% of Americans *feel* wealthy, and the average net worth of those who *feel* wealthy is $560,000.[2] If you look at either of those numbers on a global scale, that net worth likely puts your number in the top 1% of all people.

I could cite many statistics on net worth and income to give context as to what it means to be rich, but the numbers will change annually based on the markets and inflation, and they likely won't mean much to you, anyway.

What may matter more than the numbers for you is what my son, Logan, was alluding to… your savings and spending habits, living within your means, your goals and desires, and the ultimate purpose of your money.

---

[1] "Are You Rich? Here's What Americans Think You Need to Be Considered Wealthy." Yahoo! Finance. Accessed July 18, 2024. https://finance.yahoo.com/news/rich-heres-americans-think-considered-182847861.html.

[2] Charles Schwab modern wealth survey 2023. Accessed August 2, 2024. https://content.schwab.com/web/retail/public/about- schwab/ schwab_modern_wealth_survey_2023_findings.pdf.

If you care to do your own searches to better determine the answer to this nebulous question, just know that whatever you find, there will be people with a lot more than what you have. Just as there will be a LOT of people with a LOT less. If the absolute numbers that you research don't give you what you're looking for, you could also use a relative measure to compare your net worth against others like you.

The authors of *The Millionaire Next Door,* Thomas J. Stanley and William D. Danko, developed a formula to help us gauge our financial health relative to our income. In addition to their many learnings about millionaires, they classified them into categories to reflect their relativity and came up with these general descriptions:

- Millionaires with a high net worth—relative to their income—are prodigious accumulators of wealth (PAWs).
- Those with a net worth well below what their income suggests it should be are under accumulators of wealth (UAWs).

Their formula for determining where you stand on that relativity scale is this: Multiply your age by your income and divide that by 10, then compare the result to your net worth. If your net worth is well above the formula's result, you're a PAW. If it's well below the formula's result, you're a UAW. And, of course, if your net worth is right in line with the formula, then you're an AAW (average accumulator of wealth).

A couple, the Smiths, recently asked me, "How are we doing?" I responded by sharing the progress they're making toward their goals. But they wanted to know how they were doing compared to their community. Using the formula from the book, we calculated their combined income at $150,000 and noted their ages— they are each 55. To categorize them, we followed this formula:

$150,000 x 55 = $8,250,000
$8,250,000 ÷ 10 = $825,000.

The Smiths' net worth was significantly higher, at $1,200,000, which classifies them as prodigious accumulators of wealth (PAWs). They are doing well relative to their community of people with similar incomes.

Another couple, the Johnsons, made $400,000 and were the same age as the Smiths, 55. Their net worth was $1,800,000 (significantly higher than the Smiths). We followed the same formula to arrive at their conclusion.

$400,000 x 55 = $22,000,000
$22,000,000 ÷ 10 = $2,200,000

With this information, we know that the Johnsons fell short of the relativity target for similar incomes and are under accumulators of wealth (UAW). Even though their net worth was higher than the Smith's net worth, the Johnsons were not on track for their own situation, and that's the most relevant comparison each of us needs to make.

There's a lot more to unpack in *The Millionaire Next Door,* and I encourage you to check out this book. But what I love is that my 13-year-old could nail the concept without research, formulas, or a book. Logan instinctively knew that not only net worth or income will determine if you're financially rich. It's *your income, relative to what you want to do and buy, that gives you the feeling of financial security.*

Your Intentional Retirement starts with these core concepts of net worth, income, and expenses. Yet, if you stay too focused on net worth and don't create consistent income, then you likely will live a retirement of missed opportunities because you worried too much about having enough.

There is another way...You can join us and our clients and begin shifting from a net worth mindset to a net income strategy and ultimately to a net impact mentality. I'm confident you'll be able to worry less and embrace more opportunities as you increase your intentionality. So, how do you begin?

Like a game of Jeopardy, the answers come in the form of questions…

- Can your net worth produce income?
- Can that income cover what you want to do, buy, and give?
- Will the income last as long as you do, and if so, how will you direct what's left?

Before we get to the fun parts of spending, giving, and living, we need to spend some time unpacking the net worth phenomenon.

To be clear, "net worth" is a relatively simple concept. To figure out our net worth, we add up all our assets (investments, real estate, personal property, business interests) and subtract all our liabilities (mortgage(s), car loans, other debts).

When we go a couple of layers deeper, there are some important distinctions about your net worth I'd like you to consider. I'll break those into three chapters to help you evaluate the relative strength of your net worth by looking at three facets of your net worth:

1. **Don't Put All Your Eggs in One Basket.** In this chapter, we'll explore asset allocation and discuss why spreading out your money as you distribute it is more critical than when you accumulate it.

THE REAL DEFINITION OF NET WORTH

2. **Never Gonna Get It**. This chapter unpacks the next layer of net worth diversification, your asset location, and how that impacts the way the IRS sees your money.

3. **Money Can't Buy Happiness**. This third component of net worth introduces the concept of purpose, as we attach it to our net worth, and begins to explore how you can intentionally use your money.

Chapter 1
Don't Put All Your Eggs in One Basket

"Concentrating your assets can make you rich, but diversifying your assets keeps you rich."

~Unknown

Most of us have either been taught by others, or we've learned the hard way not to keep "all our eggs in one basket." Diversification means spreading out our assets between different investments in case bad things happen.

In the investment world, we typically split assets between tools like cash, bonds, and stocks. We might also add other assets like real estate (your primary residence or vacation homes) and business interests. Some people have illiquid investments, such as income-producing tools like pensions, annuities, loans to family and friends, and rental properties, while others keep their money in liquid, flexible places like savings or money market accounts. All these options are great, and all have their drawbacks. There are, of course, many ways to invest our money, and we need to evaluate the pros/cons of each and calculate the risk/return tradeoffs that we're willing to accept.

This process is commonly referred to as "asset allocation," and it's geared toward your risk profile, goals, and timeframe for when you'll use your money. You've likely completed questionnaires and had conversations about this as you've invested through the years. Perhaps you've labeled yourself conservative, moderate, or aggressive. These are helpful terms to describe a mentality, but I would argue that you should remove whatever label you've worn while you have been *accumulating* your money.

Let me elaborate...

During the accumulation phase of your life (which you may still be in if you're working), you had income covering your expenses and very little need to withdraw money (outside of larger planned expenses like a vacation or project and unexpected emergencies), and hopefully, these withdrawals came from an emergency fund or savings accounts. Your other assets might've gone up and down in the markets (generally up), and when they went down, you hopefully:

a. Didn't look at the statements
b. Worried a little and moved on
c. Bought more of those investments (think payroll contributions to your 401k).

If you had good investments that were unlikely to go to zero (such as shares of an index fund), it was probable that you could hold them or buy more, and they'd eventually go back up—so this strategy would've worked. Thus, we know that asset allocation doesn't matter as much as when you are accumulating money—when it's easier to be aggressive.

In retirement, your entire net worth is your "emergency" fund. That's because you're in the "distribution" phase (as opposed to the "accumulation" phase), and you need to regularly take out money so you can use it to spend, give, and live. There's no longer a paycheck to support you during the bad market cycles. Now, instead of investing more into the market to buy more shares when they're down in value, you're doing the opposite... Selling more shares (because they're down in value) to get the amount of money you need to live. In turn, those shares aren't part of your net worth, and they don't have a chance to recover in value because they've been spent. Now, let's over-simplify this complexity to better understand the serious difference.

Accumulation

Accumulation is a simple concept. It just means that you keep buying when the market drops. For example:

You invest $1,000/month and buy XYZ index for $100/share, which means you add 10 shares/month to your portfolio.

Then…

The market drops, and XYZ fund is down 20% to $80/share.

If you keep buying, you add 12.5 shares/month to your portfolio.

If…

The market eventually recovers after 12 months, and XYZ goes back to $100/share, so the market is *even with where it started, d*o you have:

a. The same amount of money you invested?
b. Less than you started with?
c. More than you started with?

Keep on thinking about it; the answer is coming in the next section.

Distribution

Distribution is another simple concept. You need money to live on and must sell when the market drops. Let's assume:

You have $100,000 in XYZ fund, it's worth $100/share, and you own 1,000 shares.

You need $1,000/month to live, so you sell 10

shares each month. You sold 120 shares. Assuming the value didn't change, you now have $88,000 after one year.

Then…

On the first day of the second year, the market drops 20%, and your shares are worth $80/share. You still need $1,000/month. You now must sell 12.5 shares/month to equate to your income goal.

Thankfully, the market jumps back up on the last day of the year and your shares are worth $100/share again, meaning that the market is even *with where it started*. Do you have:

a. $76,000 (because you took out 2 years of $12,000, and the share price is the same)?
b. More than $76,000 (because the market recovered in the second year)?
c. Less than $76,000 (because you sold more shares to get the same income)?

If you answered "c" to both the accumulation and distribution questions, you are correct.

Strangely enough, a down market can equal good fortune while you're accumulating money. But when you're distributing money each month to live on, a down market can wreak havoc on your investments.

Hopefully, these scenarios help to illustrate the severe impact that market ups and downs will have on your net worth during your distribution phase. We'll discuss ways to navigate these events in the chapters on "net income." For now, I'd like you to think about this concept:

Asset allocation, as part of an intentional retirement, means rethinking your assets and attaching purpose to each piece of your puzzle. It also means discerning an important distinction— what parts of your net worth are assets, and what parts are investable or income-producing assets.

As an example, which of these couples is likely better prepared for retirement?

1. Todd and Mary have a net worth of44 $2,000,000 comprised of:
2.
   a. $600,000 home (no debt)
   b. $400,000 vacation home (no debt)
   c. $150,000 in cars, jewelry, and other personal assets
   d. $800,000 in stocks and mutual funds in retirement accounts
   e. $50,000 in checking and savings (not individual retirement accounts; non-IRAs)

3. Bill and Hillary have a net worth of $2,000,000, comprised of:

    a. $600,000 home (no debt)
    b. $400,000 rental property (no debt)
    c. $800,000 in stocks and mutual funds and bonds in retirement accounts
    d. $200,000 in stocks, mutual funds, savings, and checking (non-IRA)

Answer: Although each couple has the same net worth, I would argue that Bill and Hillary have a much stronger retirement net worth because they have a higher percentage of investable assets. Said differently, Bill and Hillary can generate income from their $400,000 property and from their more significant amount of non-IRA assets.

Todd and Mary can, of course, enjoy their vacation home, cars, and jewelry, but they have *obligations* instead of *investments* as part of their asset allocation.

I realize this is a somewhat basic example, but distinguishing the purpose of an asset is so critical when you track your net worth and your asset allocation in preparation for retirement.

Your vacation home, cars, and jewelry all require maintenance and insurance, as well as other associated costs. They are wonderful to have but arguably shouldn't be counted in your asset allocation for retirement net worth purposes.

Please know I'm not suggesting that you don't acquire or enjoy any of those items. I'm simply suggesting that when you track your asset allocation for retirement, you consider these questions:

- Can you use the asset for income?
- Will you need to withdraw some of the value from that asset to help with your living expenses?
- Will that withdrawal be soon or years down the road?
- Can you hold the asset long enough to endure the market's ups and downs?

We've all heard the horror stories of people who have lost everything from a bad investment or even from bad timing with a good investment.

I'll spare you the sob stories and the scary admonishments and share an alternative view instead: You don't NEED to use asset allocation for your accumulation or distribution years.

A Non-traditional Route

Roger and Karen retired in their early fifties from corporate careers. Karen was successful at a telecom company and escaped with some money intact after the tech bubble burst in the early 2000s. Despite seeing many colleagues lose nearly everything in companies that went bust, Roger and Karen went against conventional wisdom and concentrated their portfolios in only a few stocks. They started IRA withdrawals early (through a specific IRS strategy that allows for substantially equal periodic payments), began Social Security early, never moved their money toward conservative investments, and continued to hold a concentrated portfolio of a few stocks.

Now in their seventies, they are living happily, having used a lot from their IRA portfolio, although the balance is still hovering around where it started: $1,000,000. Their plan was helped by a small defined-benefit pension (that's paid to them like a monthly income) and a modest inheritance that Roger received, but mainly, they've rolled the dice and won!

Why do I share their story?

I want you to know that you don't have to take a traditional route. It's your life. But beware, for each "Roger and Karen" out there, I could provide 10 times as many stories that didn't work out.

Because of the risk/reward tradeoff and the boom/bust scenarios, most people prefer to mitigate risk.

A more typical approach is to spread out investments between different types of assets to preserve and protect some money while allocating other amounts to provide growth opportunities. These are the stories we'll focus on to create an Intentional Retirement.

Before we move our attention fully to retirement, let me share some advice and perspectives applicable if you are still accumulating money. I wrote the following article about investing during COVID, but I believe it's still relevant today:

Quick...make a guess! How many boxes of cereal did my family eat in March?

Four boys (ages 9-14), plus my wife and me...and a shelter-in-place order for half the month...did you guess?

And does it matter?

Of course, it doesn't really matter, but we went through 25 boxes. And we were just getting warmed up... April's numbers will blow that away. Some boxes of Fruity Pebbles or Lucky Charms were small, and some Frosted Flakes and Apple Jacks were family-size bulk boxes, and there was everything in between. Yet, they all had one thing in common, and that is what's relevant for you.

The common bond I'm referring to is not that they are rotting our teeth but rather that they were all bought on sale. And that made me think about the stock market...

What Do Cereal and Stocks Have to Do with Each Other?

You can buy them both for the long haul! Cereal, for the most part, doesn't really go bad when un-opened. So, we buy lots of different kinds (even the "favorites" go out of favor after a while) when they go on sale... We know we can put them on the shelf and wait until we need them later.

Many of our clients are asking us now if they should buy certain stocks or add more money into the market. We have lots of data, plenty of technical ways to decide, plus great research and resources to make informed decisions. And yet, we don't exactly know.

We can help plan and buy more for the long haul, but no one has ever experienced what's happening right now!

My family doesn't buy vegetables the same way we buy cereal (on sale and in bulk) as vegetables can go bad quickly and become worthless, so we buy them in smaller quantities.

Perhaps the same principles may apply to the market. Through lots of "unprecedented" times during the last 100-plus years, the market has never gone to zero, but many companies have disappeared along the way.

I'm not making stock recommendations here or telling you how to invest; we should have a conversation and a plan before we do that. I'm just saying that it's usually not a bad thing to buy something you need when it's on sale. Especially when you think it won't go bad, and you know that you can put it on the shelf until you need it later.

Forget toilet paper. I'm stocking up on index funds and cereal!

If you've already transitioned from accumulation to distribution (retirement), then that story may have less impact, but the point remains: You'll still need cereal in 20-plus years, and you probably should have some money in the stock market to help your money grow so you can buy that cereal (and everything else you need) in the future.

You just want to be able to hold that money and sell at an advantageous time. But if you're also withdrawing money right now to buy your cereal (and live your life) each month, then you'll likely want to spread out your money across multiple assets, so you're not forced to sell when the markets are down.

Asset allocation, to us at IntentGen Financial Partners, means having pieces of your investable net worth that will:

- **Avoid** risk and preserve principal while providing liquidity (the ability to withdraw quickly, without losing).
- **Absorb** risk and spread it across a portfolio (a diversified mix of cash, bonds, and stocks).
- **Accept** risk and provide long-term growth potential for your investments.
- **Transfer** risk to hedge the unexpected and protect your income, preserve your assets, or more efficiently transfer your money.

In our financial planning process, the first step is to *Organize.* This seems obvious, but if you're like many people we meet, you may have pieces of your financial puzzle that you haven't looked at in years. It's important to take inventory. When my team and I help people finally look at everything together, we find most frequently that although people have diversified their investments across companies, *they often hold the same assets in multiple places.*

Meet Peter

Peter is a do-it-yourself investor, and in many ways, he has done it well. He came to meet with me and was proud that he and his wife, Cindy, had amassed a net worth of over $2,000,000. He felt confident that this total would more than take care of them throughout their retirement.

He arrived at that conclusion using the 4% rule[3], a generally accepted theory (see additional comments and disclosures) around retirement planning, positing if you use 4% of your account's value each year, you should be able to keep up with inflation and have your money last through retirement.

Peter combined his $80,000 income (4% of $2,000,000) with his and Cindy's Social Security and felt comfortable with the results to cover his anticipated living expenses.

Peter felt good that he had spread out his risk so that if any one company that he trusted had a problem, his risk would be mitigated. He accomplished this by holding funds with most of the big brokerage companies.

---

[3] Despite an on-going debate about this 4% approach and what percent is statistically reasonable, I am neither debating, denying, or advocating it. I'm simply saying that this was Peter's theory and approach (although he had no plan for how to withdraw money, from a practical standpoint).

However, when we looked "under the hood" at his portfolio, I quickly observed that although Peter held his money at four different companies, most of it was in large cap stocks through S&P 500 index funds and several mutual funds. This has served Peter well over the last 10 years, but historically, it adds a tremendous amount of risk.

When I pointed out that Peter held the exact same fund in two different accounts, even though one was at Schwab and one was at Fidelity, he was even more surprised. (This happens quite often because these firms are "custodians" that can custody/hold many of the same investments.) Peter realized that he was missing many pieces of the investment pie and is currently evaluating alternatives to help prepare him and Cindy for when they need to distribute money to live on.

As reasonable as it is for us to assume that Peter's large cap stock investments and index funds can earn more than 4% over time, it is not reasonable to assume that each year will provide positive returns.

Think about the accumulation/distribution examples I've shared and how that will impact Peter when the market declines at some point. Peter has invested and accumulated very well, but he is not diversified across asset allocation for the distribution phase. Perhaps the order of market returns will be favorable for Peter like it was for Roger and Karen, and his plan will work well.

I have worked through the crazy markets of '00-'02, '07-'09, and '20 and '22, and unless you really like to gamble, I don't want you to take the risk of being forced to sell your investments to meet your living expenses during a bear market.

You may feel that these descriptions of asset allocation are too simple, or maybe you're tempted to quit reading this section because it was too technical for you. Without a doubt, asset allocation is a complex puzzle and a topic best handled on an individual basis, based on your situation.

The simplest way I can break down asset allocation is that you probably should have multiple investments (cash, bonds, stocks, annuities, real estate, business interests) in your portfolio as you retire, and if they can produce income, then they really count.

Have fun tracking your overall net worth, but begin to narrow your retirement net worth to include only investable assets' pieces.

Now, let's move on, because asset allocation is just step one of having a net worth ready for an intentional retirement!

Retire Intentionally Exercises

At the end of each chapter, you will find an action or exercise to help you on your journey. Let's get started exploring how you are positioned for retirement. Please access www.retire-intentionally.com to complete your:

1. Assets Risk Tolerance Questionnaire
2. Investable Assets Net Worth Summary

Scan for end of chapter worksheets or visit Retire-Intentionally.com

Chapter 2
Never Gonna Get It

"You must pay taxes. But there's no law that says you gotta leave a tip."

~Morgan Stanley

What two things are certain in life? Death and taxes, of course! These two topics are integral to finding the ideal location for your assets. We define asset location by splitting your investments into three categories, so you can look at your money the way the IRS does. That means you must know when taxes are due.

As critical as your diversification is across the asset allocation spectrum that we just covered, it is perhaps even more important to diversify your assets across the tax spectrum.

Your Tax Efficiency Checklist

As you track your net worth and the values of your investable assets, try to answer these questions to determine the tax impact for each piece of your financial puzzle:

a. Do you get taxed on the gains of your money each year as it grows?
b. Do you get taxed on the gains later when you sell the investment or withdraw it?
c. Do you never* get taxed on the money?

*if used properly, tools like ROTH IRAs, life insurance, ROTH 401ks, and 529s will never be taxed

Remember Peter and Cindy and their $2,000,000 net worth? If you recall, it was mostly allocated to large cap stocks. When I dug one level deeper into their portfolio, I observed that about 10% of their money was in a non-IRA brokerage account (with about half of it split into money markets and CDs and half in an S&P 500 index fund). About 80% of their money was in IRAs and his current retirement plan. The final 10% was split between a ROTH IRA (mostly cash) and an insurance policy.

Before we go any further, I want to underscore that this book isn't meant to be a tax guide or explain all the technical aspects of each category. However, there are some basic tax concepts that are critical to understand. I am inserting a chart below that we use as a planning tool and progress report for our clients. We call it the *Tax Efficiency Checklist (TEC)**, and

---

*Thrivent Tax Efficiency Checklist (TEC) is © 2024 Thrivent, used with permission.

we have borrowed it with permission from Thrivent Financial and used it with clients for decades. This tool helps them look at their money the way the IRS does (how and when does it get taxed?) and through the lenses of asset allocation, asset location, and purpose.

TAX NOW (see disclosures)		TAX LATER (see disclosures)		TAX NEVER (see disclosures)	
Amount	Purpose	Amount	Purpose	Amount	Purpose
Checking[1]		IRAs[2,3,4]		Roth IRAs[4,5]	
Savings[1]		401(k)[2,3,4]		Roth 401(k)[4,5]	
CDs[1]		403(b) and other retirement[2,3,4]		Municipal Bonds[1,6]	
Mutual Funds[1]		Variable Annuities[3,4]		Life Insurance Cash Value[4,7]	
Stocks (Dividends)[1]		Fixed Annuities[3,4]		529 College Savings Plans[5]	
Bonds[1]		Stocks[1] (Capital Gains)		Health Savings Accounts (H.S.A.)[5]	
Other		Other		Other	
Total		Total		Total	
0		0		0	
Investable Assets Total	0				

Peter, like many people, has learned and been coached to invest in large cap stocks through pre-tax retirement plans (401ks and 403bs are the most common examples). While these are great during the accumulation phase of our lives and are "diversified" with different companies, they provide less than the ideal amount of tax diversification for someone ready to retire and draw income. Furthermore, pre-tax retirement accounts are not optimal for the beneficiaries of Peter's account (his children are in a higher tax-bracket than him) because they will be required to pay income tax on the deferred growth. (We'll spend more time exploring passing on assets in later chapters.) Now, let's talk about why the location of their assets matters to Peter and Cindy.

TAX NOW (see disclosures)		TAX LATER (see disclosures)		TAX NEVER (see disclosures)	
Amount	Purpose	Amount	Purpose	Amount	Purpose
Checking $ 10,000		IRAs $ 400,000		Roth IRAs $ 150,000	
Savings		401(k) $ 1,200,000		Roth 401(k)	
CDs $ 100,000		403(b) and other retirement		Municipal Bonds	
Mutual Funds $ 100,000		Variable Annuities		Life Insurance Cash Value $ 50,000	
Stocks (Dividends)		Fixed Annuities		529 College Savings Plans	
Bonds		Stocks (Capital Gains)		Health Savings Accounts (H.S.A.)	
Other		Other		Other	
Total		Total		Total	
$ 210,000		$ 1,600,000		$ 200,000	
Investable Assets Total	$ 2,010,000				

Imagine that you made a smart investment, and it has grown incredibly. Would you rather own it in a brokerage account, a 401k, or a ROTH IRA? Let's say you got lucky and bought Apple, Amazon, or an index fund at just the right time, and you'd invested $10,000. That $10,000 is now worth $30,000, and you're ready to start using it.

If it's in a 401k (middle column on the aforementioned TEC) and you're not yet 59 ½, your employer and the government impose restrictions. You may have to pay a 10% federal penalty upon withdrawing, that is, if your company even allows the distribution. Regardless of the pre-59 ½ rules, you will most certainly pay taxes on your $20,000 gain at a marginal tax rate of 10-37% (based on your total income), plus some states will tax you on this retirement distribution. Finally, if you added to your 401k pre-tax (as most contributions are set up), then you'll pay tax on the original $10,000 deposit.

If you're past 59 ½, the 10% penalty doesn't apply, but your employer's rules still do. You can get past those employer rules in many cases by doing a tax-free rollover to your own individual retirement account (IRA), but that brings in lots of other issues to consider (costs, investment management, etc.). And, if you're around age 73, make sure you start withdrawing because you must take a required minimum distribution (RMD—keep reading for more on that) each year from your IRA.

If you owned that same investment in a brokerage account (also the middle column on the TEC), you can sell it to use whenever you want and pay capital gains taxes. Your tax rate will be 0%, 15%, or 20%, plus the potential of an additional 3.8% Medicare tax (if your income goes above $250,000, married filing jointly), and don't forget that most states will tax you on the capital gain. If you collected dividends on that investment along the way, you will have had to pay taxes on those as you go (refer to the left column of the TEC).

But you're smarter than that, right? You made that investment in a ROTH IRA (right column on the TEC). You deferred the taxes along the way, and now you can sell it and pay no taxes at all—if you're older than 59 ½. There's just a small catch... you probably didn't invest that $10,000 in a ROTH IRA because you've never been able to *contribute* that much in a given year due to the fact that there are maximum contribution limits that change each year (as of 2024, the limit is $7,000 for people under 50 and $8,000 for people 50 and over). Plus, if your income was too high and/or you had a retirement plan through work, you couldn't contribute at all. There are other ways to get money into a ROTH (taxable conversions from IRA to ROTH and back-door conversions of non-deductible IRAs to ROTHs; consult your financial and tax advisor about both scenarios to see if they make sense for you).

Phew... are you lost yet?
Confused?
Exhausted?

Diversify Your Money for Tax Reasons

That was just one simple (very confusing) explanation of why it matters to have your money diversified in different locations with respect to taxes.

In short, tax deferral is good. Until it's not. And then, maybe it is... I could recount countless stories and case studies on how people have intentionally minimized taxes or accidentally maximized their taxes (not good). But these stories would likely just confuse the topic even more. It's an incredibly complex section, so take a breather. We'll dig into it again later in the book.

Now, how about some simplicity to wrap up this

complexity? I'll close out this asset location section with a few general comments. As you read along, please bear in mind that, as always, I'm not giving you tax advice but rather sharing some general observations:

During retirement, you have more control than ever over which tax bracket you're in (when you work and earn income, that is the major driver of your tax bracket; when you're drawing money out, you choose how much, from which investment, and when to take it). These are critical decisions that will help define an Intentional Retirement.

1. Having money in multiple asset classes across all three columns gives you even greater flexibility to decide where to take from so you can better manage your tax bracket in retirement.
2. If you're not yet retired, you can do a lot to save in different locations leading up to retirement. If you are retired, it's not over yet... You have many options in the years ahead. You can think about the tax impact over your lifetime, and beyond, not just look at whether you had to pay the IRS or got a refund on a year-to-year basis.

This last observation supports the perspective on devising an intentional net worth... which has everything to do with purpose!

Retire Intentionally Exercise

Your next step to better understand your potential retirement scenario is to visit www.retire-intentionally.com and complete:

1. Your Tax-Efficiency Checklist

Scan for end of chapter worksheets or visit Retire-Intentionally.com

Chapter 3
Money Can't Buy Happiness

"Life isn't about money. It's about moments."
~David Castain

Net worth is simple to calculate, but oh, is it complex. We track it. We try to grow it. And we compare it (to where we were in the past and to others). We might feel good about it at times, and we certainly feel terrible about it at other times (like when the stock market or real estate markets are down).

Time after time, clients have entrusted me with the net worth number they're shooting for, whether that be $1,000,000, $3,000,000, or $10,000,000. "If I can just get to that number," they say, "then I will have enough. We will be secure."

Through the years, I've observed that when the achievement-minded people I've worked with accomplish their aspirations, they have typically done so by:

- Setting goals
- Sharing them
- Committing to them
- Creating habits to attain them

I'm happy to share that dozens of clients have set goals for aspirational net worth. Almost every client who has shared their net worth goal has reached it (this observation is a testament to them—it's not me trying to take credit for their commitment). Yet, interestingly enough, in almost every case where each person has hit their goal, they have subsequently increased it. They share sentiments like: "Even though I got to three million, I'd truly be fine if I got to four million!"

Why is that?

Maybe it's because they've compared themselves to others. Perhaps they thought of more things they'd like to do. Maybe inflation caused them to realize their number just isn't what it used to be! More than likely, it's because they worried about more things that could go wrong. And maybe, just maybe, it's because they simply want more.

Let me be clear: There's nothing wrong with more…Please know, in this book, I'm not trying to tell anyone how to live their life or how to spend/save/give their money. If you want the biggest net worth possible, then go build it. If you want to give all your net worth away, then go do it. Just do it intentionally with purpose and confidence.

I've heard about every possible scenario and story from people regarding their net worth and its purposes. Duane is just one such client.

Scarcity Mindset

I've worked with Duane for many years. He has a net worth over $1,000,000 and continually jokes that he and his family "just don't want to eat dog food or live in a box under a bridge." The joke wasn't that funny the first time I heard it, and it's really not funny 15 years later. It's also just a cover-up for the real issue, which is that Duane doesn't have a defined purpose for his money. He and his wife have more than enough for themselves, but an attitude of scarcity (worrying about having enough) and a lack of purpose for the money (they don't really go anywhere, do much with family or friends, or give to charities) means that their net worth just floats up and down, and their worries continue.

Duane is not alone in this mindset. I have done a thorough analysis of income sources, fixed and variable expenses, asset allocation, tax-efficiency, and probable longevity for many people just like Duane and his wife, and it is abundantly clear that they have enough. Yet they're unwilling to do much because they're attached to the $1,000,000 figure on their net worth statement and hate the idea of seeing it go below that.

Other people joke that they want to "spend it all" and have their last check bounce. If that is your goal and your purpose, there is a way to accomplish that with your net worth. You could transition your money into a series of lifetime annuity payments that will pay you money every month as long as you live and then leave nothing at the end. Nobody that I know has chosen that strategy, but it is possible!

All joking aside, your net worth is a serious subject! There is a danger, though, in just measuring net worth for the sake of measurement. Without context, we get caught up in the numbers on paper, and we don't know how they affect our lives.

Measuring from the Top

Stanley has a significant net worth that he has tracked carefully for years. Part of why he regularly watches it stems from his financial career. It was his job to track finances and make financial decisions for the companies he worked for. Another part of why he watches it closely is because he remembers a time when his net worth was basically zero. It feels good to him to see that number so high. Stanley and his wife have saved diligently and prepared well for retirement. Then, in early 2020, shortly after Stanley retired, he watched his net worth drop by over 20% within a couple of weeks as the COVID crisis shocked the world and rattled stock markets.

Our company was never busier than during those first months of COVID. We reminded people of their plans and strategies, and we tried to help them remove emotion from their decisions. Still, Stanley's review meeting on Zoom was different than most others…His net worth was precariously close to a number he couldn't stand to see breached, and he was determined not to see it go below that line that he had mentally drawn.

Stanley knew that he didn't need the money to live on because he and his wife had other savings and income, yet he decided to eliminate more risk and sell his investments because he couldn't bear the thought of his net worth going any lower. In hindsight, was that the right decision?

That's an impossible question for you or me to answer because we don't control Stanley's money, and we don't live his life. Stanley and I still talk and meet regularly, and he realizes what he could have earned back as the market has rebounded in the months and years since then. But he also knows the situation could've been much different. He's made peace with his decision and is grateful that he hasn't had to endure some of the stresses that the market has brought to many people since then. Preserving his net worth and protecting his capital was his primary objective, and he accomplished that.

Stanley has also gained additional perspective during these early years of his retirement that I think will help shape his and his wife's next 20 or 30 years:

They don't *live on* their net worth. Net worth is, in fact, just a number on paper. Stanley and his wife actually *live off* their income, meaning they spend, give, and live from their consistent income, even as their net worth fluctuates. They are now having more fun exploring what their *net worth's purpose* will be rather than worrying about the number.

The purpose of investments is such a critical component of our assets that it gets the biggest section on the Tax Efficiency Checklist that we covered in the previous chapter.

It's also hopefully the most fun part to talk about when it comes to your investment portfolio. Purpose essentially boils down to a few main questions:

1. Are you going to spend it? If so... will you spend it soon or down the road?
   a. Will you need it for regular monthly income?
   b. Will you withdraw it as periodic lump sums?
2. Are you going to give it? If so...
   a. Will you give it during your life?
   b. Will you give it to people (family and/or friends)?
   c. Will you give it to places (church and/or charities)?
3. If you're not sure about whether you'll spend it or give it, then you're essentially saving it.

What are you saving it for?

    a. Is this "what if" money? E.g., "What if I need it for healthcare, to help family, or something else?"

    b. Is this more fun money for you?

    c. Is it eventually going to people (kids, grandkids, family, and/or friends)?

    d. Is it eventually going to places (non-profits or other institutions)?

Once you define the purpose, it is much easier to figure out which asset allocation and asset location types are appropriate. With that confidence, you can then select the most appropriate type of investment vehicle from the checklist. As a blanket disclaimer, each of the options on the list has bad properties as well as good. A fiduciary (someone who's acting in your best interest) advisor who has access to all those possibilities is likely your best partner for figuring out these choices. And, although listed last in this section, the purpose of your assets is really the first conversation you should have.

A Unique Example of a Common Concern

David's most important asset is a vacation home that has been in his family for generations. David and his wife, Cheree, understand purpose and have used that word to prioritize this period of their life. They have been retired for a few years, although he doesn't like the word retired... "You just stay busy in other things," he says. He and Cheree focus on family and giving back and split time between the US and Switzerland, where they grew up. They want their home in Switzerland to stay in the family for generations to come and although it holds great memories and offers fun opportunities for the future, it also requires considerable money to maintain and operate each year. David and Cheree love their ski chalet in the Swiss Alps, and it's a big part of their overall net worth. Although most people don't have the luxury (or the responsibility) of thinking about a family ski chalet in the Alps, our company regularly works with people thinking about similar transitions for a family lake house, vacation home, farmland, or even their primary residence.

David shared with me that he has tried to take some of the guesswork out of their planning. He looked at his key uncertainties (longevity and maintaining properties in two different countries) and modeled scenarios of what could happen. His perspective has been not to worry about being precise (and inevitably wrong) but for his projections to be approximately right. He focused on income first. Once he and Cheree had confidence in their regular income, they could focus on the vacation home and the purpose of their other investments.

They also think about how that home will need to be shared by their children and their families, who have different incomes and financial resources. Because they want those families to share in the joy without causing unnecessary financial stress, they've already been re-purposing assets to pass on tax-efficiently and provide liquidity to the next generations. Investment options like ROTH IRAs, life insurance, and marketable investments (like stocks) that receive a "step-up" in cost basis at death (under current tax law) are all ideal to align with their purpose.

Each of these options also has its risks and drawbacks, but the primary purpose of transitioning the family's vacation home means they can evaluate the tradeoffs. For them, paying taxes on money now to convert to a ROTH is a great strategy because it aligns with their purpose.

It's Just Eric

Eric is a client and friend in his seventies. He had a great business career, managed his money well, and inherited a significant amount from his parents. Eric never had children, married later in life, and was widowed way too early in retirement! Philanthropy is very important to Eric and his brother, who also inherited money. The purpose of money, for Eric, beyond the regular income he needs to enjoy life, is to give and grow the money throughout his lifetime and maximize the amount he can give to charity at the end of it.

The investment options Eric uses look very different than the tools David uses. Eric takes advantage of tax-deferred annuities for money that he doesn't need because it minimizes current income, interest, and capital gains and keeps his taxable income lower (which reduces his Medicare income penalty-IRMAA[4] and allows him to reallocate investments without tax implications). It also means that all his gains are tax-deferred for somebody else to pay. In this case, that somebody else is a non-profit organization that doesn't pay income taxes. As much as Eric likes ROTH IRAs for himself, it makes little sense to convert from an IRA to a ROTH because it would increase his current tax burden and send tax-free money at his death to an organization that doesn't pay tax.

Each of these examples helps illustrate the critical importance of attaching purpose and aligning your priorities with your money. If you only use a spreadsheet to track your net worth number, you are missing a big part of the equation.

---

[4] In short, the higher your income, the more you're going to pay for Medicare. IRMAA refers to Income-Related Monthly Adjustment Amount—a surcharge on Medicare Part B and Part D premiums based on a person's modified adjusted gross income.

Although net worth is an important number to track, it doesn't encompass nearly the entirety of our financial situations, let alone our lives. I've learned from clients over the years to consider adding a few additional columns to net worth statements to help make a more complete picture.

More Than Numbers

Julie is a client who has had an incredibly successful banking career. By her own admission, at times, there have been career choices that have had a negative impact on her family life. She has gone through a divorce, yet is still close to her kids and is proud that she helped them through college while she also rebuilt her own financial situation. As she tracked her financial progress, Julie realized through our ongoing planning conversations that she was missing out on some experiences and opportunities that mattered to her.

During a recent review meeting, Julie shared that she added a new column to her balance sheet that she titled "JOY." She started to track financial changes (such as selling her existing home and buying a new home) that better fit her lifestyle. She also planned and invested in some major trips with friends.

Although these were all changes that prevented her net worth from going up as fast, they brought more joy to her life than numbers on paper. She found it valuable to track her milestones as well as her numbers.

Todd is another client who helped me learn about tracking net worth. He used Excel to create a spreadsheet with a rolling "graph" to show the progress of his assets, liabilities, and net worth over time. It was fascinating to look back at the ups and downs throughout a long period. It captured the trends and the numbers, but from my perspective, it didn't capture any impact. I now use a similar version, but I added a column that matters to me. Charitable giving is my wife's and my top financial priority. The money we give annually to non- profit organizations is a bigger amount than any of our other categories (e.g., housing, cars, hobbies, kids' activities, credit cards, vacations, etc.), and I wanted to track the long-term impact. Now, with an annual and cumulative giving column on my net worth statement, I see the year-to-year progress of how much we're giving. It also allows us to visualize the rolling and cumulative effects of how our income and net worth can help us impact the people and places we care about.

What Do You Value?

Say what you will, but the financial proof is likely in your bank and credit card statements. I encourage you to review where your money has gone and where it is going. It will tell you a lot about what you value. If your money isn't lined up with what you thought you valued, then perhaps finding a way to track that on your net worth statement will help you align your priorities with your finances.

Yes, your net worth matters. But remember that it is just a number. And, although nearly all of us care what our number is, nobody else really does. Does anyone other than your financial advisor, accountant, or attorney ever ask you for it? If they did, would you tell them? I've been to a lot of funerals, and I've never seen a net worth number in a casket or obituary.

The solid foundation of your Intentional Retirement will be solidified only as your net worth is re-aligned through *asset allocation, asset location, and aligning purpose* with each piece of the puzzle. By doing this, we can free ourselves from the number on paper and focus on how we'll use it. From this strong base, we can shift from the fluctuations of a net worth number to the importance of a net income mindset.

Retire Intentionally Exercise

I love this next step in discovering where my purpose can help others and bring me more fulfillment. I know you will, too. Head to www.retire-intentionally.com to complete your own list of where you can contribute charitable gifts, joy, experiences, or make an impact (think projects, gifts to kids, grandchildren's college funds, etc.).

Scan for end of chapter worksheets or visit Retire-Intentionally.com

Net Income

Nothing but Net

"The hardest thing to understand in the world is income tax."
~Albert Einstein

B y the simplest of definitions, net income is easy to understand. It's what's left when you add up your income sources and subtract taxes. But when I ask people what their net income is, most people don't know.

How much do you make? It's a relatively simple question, and yet challenging for most people to answer! The good news is, in this section, I am going to help you answer that question.

Remember that I told you some sections would get a little technical? Stay with me, please, because the following pages contain the most important concepts for you to maximize your ability to spend and give your money while also minimizing your taxes.

Back to our question of how to calculate net income. The reason why this can be so tough is because it has so many different meanings to different people. Additionally, terms are often used interchangeably, although they don't mean the same thing.

1. What is your gross (before taxes) income?
2. What is your net (after taxes) income?
3. What is your net deposit (after taxes, 401k, and any other deductions are withdrawn)?

This *net deposit* number is likely the most important for you to focus on, because that's what you are able to use each month. But it doesn't tell the whole story.

What occurred before you even got your *gross income*? That's what you need to know.

Does your employer pay part of your healthcare?
Do they provide you with benefits like a car, internet, or cell phone?

And do you ever get bonuses, stock options, or some other incentive that is not part of your normal cash flow routine?

To get an accurate depiction of what you need and want to spend in retirement, these are questions that need to be answered. To progressively tackle this complex and most critical component of your intentional retirement, I need to break this topic into three chapters:

1. **I Hate Budgets!** In this chapter, we'll address some big questions, like "How much do you

spend on a Saturday?" and "What's your marginal tax bracket?" We'll unpack how you literally—using cash, credit cards, and bank accounts—spend your money.

2. **Live Long and Prosper.** This second chapter focuses on net income and explores ways to create cash flow when your paycheck stops. We'll also discuss ways to make sure your income lasts as long as you do.

3. **Maximize Your Money.** The third chapter introduces concepts to minimize unnecessary risks, fees, and taxes to maximize opportunities.

Although this section may feel complex, my goal is to simplify it by helping you think about how you want to use your money. I encourage you to focus on the dollars you will use, and partner with professionals to help navigate the complexities of taxes and inflation.

Chapter 4
I Hate Budgets

"A budget tells us what we can't afford, but it doesn't keep us from buying it."
~William Feather

Although calculating net income feels messy and taxes may seem too technical to fully understand, they are important to think about as you retire because they correspond with the most critical cash flow question for your retirement:

How Much Do You Spend on a Saturday?

In some ways, your retirement life is about to turn into a whole bunch of Saturdays, so you must be able to answer this question.

On your ideal weekend, do you enjoy golfing, shopping, theater, dining out, concerts, sporting events, traveling, or other activities that cost a lot? Or do you prefer reading, exercising, volunteering, gardening, or other activities that cost very little? Regardless of how you spend your time, your activities within each category can vary wildly. Travel means very different experiences to different people, for instance, and even something simple like exercise can cost almost nothing (walking/running), or it can cost a lot if you have trainers or expensive equipment.

I vividly remember an evening when I was a teenager. My mom was forcing me to do the dishes, and I was pleading to be done with them while simultaneously begging for a new pair of shoes and shorts that I *needed* to have for basketball. Those shoes and shorts were nearly $100 (in 1992), but I didn't have the context of how that fit into their finances. I didn't know how much money my parents made, but I knew they were careful with their money—this allowed them to give generously to our church and provide a great life for my two brothers and me. I learned quickly that the shoes and shorts were more than my parents wanted to allocate toward the clothing budget when my Mom denied my request and sarcastically responded: "You better get a good job because you *really* like nice things!"

I took that advice to heart…

Fast-forward 30 years from that night of dirty dishes and denied requests… In 2022, I planned out a two-month sabbatical from my company. It was a period to Stop. Rest. Delight. Contemplate. If you're curious to learn more about my adventures, search "Zac Larson Sabbatical" on YouTube and check out three videos: One from before the sabbatical and two from after the experience.

The point of sharing this is that my sabbatical period gave me important insights into key components of retirement life, and it reinforced what my mom told me in 1992. Not only do I like nice things, but I like *to do* expensive things.

My hobbies include golfing, cycling, sporting events, skiing, scuba diving, and traveling in style. These hobbies are not my life…My life revolves around what I value most: Family time, meaningful work, volunteering, and serving. That's much more important than my hobbies, and I spend more time on what I value. But when I'm not engaged in those areas of my life, chances are I'm spending time and money on my hobbies.

To compound this financial need, I also value giving money to charitable organizations as much or more than I value giving my time to them. My sabbatical reinforced these needs for me and helped me realize that I had to re-work some of my retirement spending assumptions.

How about you? What do you value?
How do you spend your money?

And how do you spend your time and money on Saturdays when you're not working?

If you can't really focus on these questions, maybe you're still thinking about your net worth number? Maybe you're thinking about how much you can spend as a function of your net worth. We already know that there are rules of thumb, like spending 4%

of your investments. Other estimates say that you'll need 80% of your income to retire comfortably. But those rules of thumb don't clarify whether your income is gross, net, or net deposit. They certainly don't take into consideration how you value spending your time and money on Saturdays.

I'd encourage you to start building your retirement cash flow through a different approach than using traditional budgets and rules of thumb. When modeling this process with our clients, we do *not* start with spreadsheets and budgets. I use both tools, but I hate them for cash flow projections because life doesn't unfold like an average on a spreadsheet. Most spending is variable and doesn't happen categorically like we've been taught to think of it (e.g., how much do you spend on groceries, clothes, entertainment, etc.?).

Perhaps you shop at Target, Costco, or Walmart. If so, do you separate your clothing, groceries, and pet food on your receipts so you can categorize how much went to each budget line? What about your vacations? Do you itemize your meals, flights, and souvenirs from your trip?

If you do... wow... I'm sorry for the people who shop and vacation with you! You're probably causing a lot of stress and compiling a lot of information that doesn't really matter. In all seriousness, *what* we spend our money on in retirement probably doesn't matter as much as *how* and *how often* we spend it.

Instead of trying to allocate your life toward traditional budget categories for money that gets used month-to-month, I encourage you instead to think of these spending methods:

1. Credit Cards
2. Cash
3. Debits

Credit Cards

Life happens! And most of what people spend as life occurs now transacts on a credit card. Thus, when I run a retirement projection for a client, I don't really care how much of their average monthly credit card is charged on groceries, clothes, wine, gas, or whatever else they value.

I just need to know the average of what you're spending on your cards each month because we need to find a way to help you pay that average each month for the rest of your life. Here's how we (and you) can go about tracking your credit card spending:

Step 1: Count the number of cards you use and log in to each account.
Step 2: Download/print your most recent *annual* spending summary for each card.
Step 3: Find the total annual spend for each card and add them together; divide that total by 12.

You now have your average monthly credit card spend.

Step 4: Gasp and recover from the shock! It's likely more than you thought.

Step 5: Stop feeling guilty, and stop defending it/rationalizing it/justifying it... for now!

Completing this exercise is critical and eye-opening. One initial reaction people have is saying something like, "But that's not normal. We had _ happen last year!"

Guess what? _____ will happen every year. It might be a different event than last year or a new change in your life, but there will always be something. New tires. New hot water heater. An unexpected trip. Doctor's bills. Helping a friend or family member.

Each new year will bring another unexpected charge, so rather than stress about it or try to budget, just go with your averages. If you want to get a better average, look back over the last 3-5 years and determine the combined average monthly total you charged on all your credit cards. My experience tells me that the only acceptable items to remove from your average credit card total are work-related travel expenses that you got reimbursed for from your employer. If you can validate additional exceptions unique to you, feel free to remove them from your total as you see fit.

Cash

Do you love the feeling of crisp $20s and $100s in your hand or wallet?

Do you still write checks?

Do you regularly take out cash or use checks to live or to give?

If so, the same principle applies to cash as it does to credit cards. It doesn't really matter what you use it for; it just matters how much and how often.

There's one important exception: If you give cash or checks to church or charity, there may be reasons you'll want to change the logistics of that gift to another method, so break that into a separate category. We'll address that later. For now, just know that if cash and checks go toward life, calculate their average monthly total and track it as a separate spending category to be added later to your average monthly credit card.

Debits

This category refers to money that people or companies take directly from your bank account. Typically, these are our bigger bills (like a mortgage, car payment, or various utilities). It might also be subscription services. As you did with the other categories, please just get the averages.

There are two important clarifications before you start tallying up your totals:

The first confusing debit is your mortgage. It's important to separate the principal and interest from taxes and insurance. This separation is significant because the principal and interest payment may continue through a portion of your retirement, but it likely will end at some point. We also don't need to "inflate" that number in retirement projections since it will stay the same each month. Your property taxes and insurance need to be tracked separately because we need to "inflate" those numbers in projections to keep up with their annual increases and to plan for how you'll pay them as lump sums when your mortgage principal is completely paid.

The second debit that trips up people is their healthcare costs because those debits often happen before you get your money. Do you know how much your private insurance is if you're pre-Medicare? Or how much your Medicare premiums are if you're

65-plus? Based on what we know about current Medicare costs and out-of-pocket costs, we can assume that most people aged 65-plus pay between $5,000-6,000/year per person for medical costs (because of IRMAA, if your income is higher, this might be more). And if you have unique healthcare needs or extra dental care, for instance, you will want to increase your projection for this debit. Typically, we'll put healthcare costs in their own category when we run a projection as we likely need to increase these expenses by a higher inflationary factor.

Now, add up your average monthly totals for credit cards, cash withdrawals, and bank debits (not counting property taxes, homeowners insurance, or healthcare). This total means you now have a handle on "normal" monthly expenses, or what I categorize as "basic living expenses." You need this money each month to live normally, so you somehow need consistent cash flow coming in to cover what's going out. In the next chapter, we'll review how to match up recurring cash flow to pay for basic or routine expenses.

This baseline we've now established allows us to begin the *fun* parts of planning: What else do you want to do, buy, or give?

Many of these categories have varying costs and are less routine. Thus, I refer to them as "periodic expenses." You might also want to think of them as "wants" or "wishes" instead of the "needs" that fall under your normal, routine expenses.

Some of these periodic categories might be travel, new cars, house projects, other large annual payments, or annual gifts to kids/grandkids. Additional categories could cover areas I already mentioned, like charitable giving, property taxes and homeowners insurance, or healthcare.

Once you have established your answers in this area, add in placeholders for any other big-ticket items that happen periodically in your life. Consider "big" trips you intentionally plan, take periodically, and remember forever. Pick a cost estimate relevant to where you want to go and who you want to take with you. These periodic categories shouldn't include smaller trips, like when you hop in the car or get on a plane to go somewhere for a few days, since that blends into the credit card spending you've already added up. The periodic expenses we're trying to capture involve activities you'd like to do during your retirement, and they start to align with *impact*.

Why would I refer to this part as *fun*?

It's fun because, at this point, we're just dreaming. You get to prioritize how you'd like to use your money and time. We don't know yet if it's financially feasible or if these expenses and experiences will last as long as you, but we get to dream together, and you get to start articulating your intentional approach to using your money for yourself, your family, your community, and the people and places you care about.

So, what else would you like to do, buy, experience, and give?

Don't Forget Your Golf Budget

James and Laurie are friends and clients I've worked with for 15 years. They value family gatherings, fun times with friends, giving money to church/charity, and serving in those same organizations. They also value and enjoy nice things and great experiences.

One of the most memorable conversations I've ever had with a client happened in a meeting with James and Laurie when we started the Prioritize phase of their retirement plan, and it was time to start dreaming. At the time, James and Laurie had already purchased a second home for retirement. We had their routine expenses locked in for our projection, but we were working at estimating some larger, periodic items. They wondered how long they could keep two homes in two different places (which also meant that they'd be keeping two country clubs and giving to two churches—one in each city).

When we added up the cost of the two country clubs, it was a much higher number than they had *estimated, amounting to about $40,000 per year for dues, meals, and other expenditures at their clubs. Then, we added up the totals for their charitable giving. Once we calculated that number, Laurie turned to her husband and said, "Don't you think our giving budget should be as high as our golf budget?"*

Before you judge any of their choices, I want to remind you...we all get to prioritize what is meaningful in our own lives.

You may think it's absurd to spend that much on golf! Someone else reading this book is thinking it's absurd to give that much money to charity. Still, someone else might think *I would never spend OR give that much.*

But we all have our stuff, like fine dining, in-app purchases on an iPhone, new cars, Amazon orders, first-class tickets, big purchases and little splurges, and on and on. I'm not suggesting what's right or wrong. I'm simply encouraging you to plan what you want to do or spend intentionally because when done accidentally, financial choices often lead to short-term happiness, which is then followed by long-term feelings of regret or guilt. When we use our money more intentionally, regretful feelings are often replaced with long-term joy because we're aligning our finances with our values.

James and Laurie talked for a minute and soon agreed that they wanted to align their finances with their values. They wanted to continue to maintain both golf memberships for a few years but also wanted to increase their charitable budget to be at least as big as their golf budget. Both were on their "wants" list and were not part of their routine credit, debit, or cash spending patterns.

With their priorities now established, we then added some "wishes" they had for helping family, although we didn't yet know if there was enough money to accomplish these hopes! We needed to figure out if it would work and how we could best get the money out of their accounts to pay for it.

We needed to know if it was more likely that they would last longer than their money, or if their money would last longer than them!

Retire Intentionally Exercise

Tracking your spending is a critical part of your retirement equation. It will tell you what you value and what you need to maintain your current expenses. And then… it will allow you to start dreaming about doing more. I've included a Cash Flow Tracker that you can fill out at www.retire-intentionally.com. Just make sure you come back here to resume reading because there's lots more to discuss!

Scan for end of chapter worksheets or visit Retire-Intentionally.com

Chapter 5
Live Long and Prosper

"If you want to live a long life, focus on making contributions."
~Hans Selye

Remember the 4% rule? This is a simple approach to help you estimate if you have enough. First, calculate your net worth and subtract assets that aren't *spendable* and don't produce income (e.g., your home). Then, multiply the remaining "investable assets" by 4%. Here's a quick refresher:

$2,600,000 net worth - minus $600,000 home = $2,000,000.

$2,000,000 x 0.04 (or 4%) = $80,000

Next, add your additional income sources, such as Social Security (SS), pension, business income, annuities, or rental income.

$40,000 SS (primary) + $20,000 SS (spousal) + $15,000 rental income = $75,000

Then, combine those numbers, and subtract an estimate for taxes:

$155,000 combined gross income - 22% average tax rate for federal and state ($34,100) = $120,900 net deposits to your checking account

This is meant to be an over-simplified example, and I realize we need to account for taxes and other cash flow issues more precisely. I'll cover that in future chapters, but for now, the point is basic cash flow: You have the capacity to receive about $10,000/month. When you compare that to your spending, do your routine expenses (needs) plus periodic spending (wants and wishes) fit within that number? If not, then there are two main levers to begin adjusting in your plan: Work longer (earn more) or decrease impact (spend less). If your early math doesn't add up, then it's time to find an advisor and start organizing, prioritizing, strategizing, and maximizing your money!

If your initial numbers look good, you're off to a great start, but there's a long way to go if you want to maximize your Intentional Retirement!

To increase your confidence that you have enough to spend, give, and live throughout your retirement, we can use better statistical models to measure the likelihood of success. Instead of relying on a "straight-line projection" (like the 4% rule, where you assume a constant rate of return, e.g., "I earn 5%/year and have a constant withdrawal rate," e.g., "I withdraw 4% and apply a constant inflation rate," e.g., "My costs go up by 3%/year)," a more advanced projection is a Monte Carlo analysis.

This term, Monte Carlo, may cause you to think of a casino, and that is, in fact, a good thought to have because, in this analysis, we're essentially reverse gambling.

This statistical approach allows us to plan for variable cash flows (which makes sense because you will likely want and need to spend different amounts in different years; think projects, vacations, cars, and gifts). It also allows us to plan for different inflation rates and prepare for variable investment returns because *they will absolutely be different in different years!*

Recall our asset allocation discussion and the example of market returns during accumulation as compared to the effects during distribution periods. You're now going to be withdrawing money each month and year, so you can use it and enjoy it. When the markets go down during your retirement, it will have a dramatically different impact on your portfolio because you're taking out money. It's critical to simulate those eventualities.

A Couple of Lucky (Planning) Ducks

Chandler and Monica have retired recently, and they have prepared well. They have been patient through ups and downs in the market and have been diligently saving through the years. In a recent planning meeting, we reviewed their retirement portfolio, and their average rate of return, after fees, had been a 7.1% annualized return for more than a decade. This means their money has more than doubled in the last 13 years because they have not withdrawn any funds.

Would it be fair to assume that they can earn 7% each year in the future? You have undoubtedly heard and read that past returns do NOT guarantee future returns.

I want to reaffirm that statement again—your past numbers are not meant to be an expectation for the future, let alone a guarantee! It is not fair to assume the 7.1% return in the future because the economy, stock market, and interest rates are all very different than they were 13 years ago. Additionally, it's not fair because we can't assume that just because something has averaged 7.1% over a long period, it will return that each year.

However, it might be fair to estimate that over a long period, a market-based portfolio *could* average 7% or more since it historically has averaged this when measured over decades. But remember, averages don't help us when we're pulling money out each year! Upon further review with Chandler and Monica, we observed that not one single year had produced a 7% return, but rather, there were lots of returns that were either much higher or lower.

The Monte Carlo analysis factors in these ups and downs that will inevitably occur in the market. It simulates potential returns based on historical market data, and as stated, it allows for changes in spending along the way, as well as accounts for inflation that will fluctuate over time. The software model then runs hundreds, if not thousands, of simulations to see if you're on track.

It sounds complex to run an analysis, and it is! In fact, Monte Carlo analysis is rocket science... It comes from the world of physics and is a very advanced way to simulate outcomes, which are used in many different fields, including rocket science. Thankfully, it's easier to review the results than it is to run the analysis!

I enjoy watching shows and movies about space travel, so I'm going to see if we can fly with this rocket science analogy a little longer.

Let's think about your retirement as a mission into space. Depending on how long you think you might live,we might be planning a shorter trip to the moon or a longer trip to Mars or beyond. To get you there, we determine the amount of necessary fuel (your net worth, and more specifically, your investable assets and income), how fast we burn it (your spending assumptions), and what cargo we're bringing (your assets, like cars and homes). Then, you can decide how much of that cargo you want to deliver when you reach your destination (essentially, you're deciding if you want to sell assets along the way or keep your assets to pass on to someone or something at your death).

In the Monte Carlo analysis, your output is simple to review because it gives you a numerical score of how many times your simulation (your current retirement plans) will work. We call this number your *probability score,* and we observe the probability of how often your retirement rocket propels you all the way through to the end of your life, e.g., in 80% of the simulations, your rocket arrives without any adjustments along the way. We also use it to calculate the probability of how much cargo (your assets and life savings) your retirement rocket can deliver to your intended targets (people and places that you care about).

There are many options to run a Monte Carlo analysis for free online, and every qualified financial advisor should use a tool like this in their planning. So, no matter where you are receiving your guidance, it shouldn't be too hard to calculate your percentage or probability of success. But this is the easy part, and it only tells you a chunk of the story. You will still need more information. Before we get to that, let me introduce you to my friends, George and Linda.

The Full-time Snowbirds

George and Linda had a strong probability for their plan early in retirement. They had moved to the south, built their retirement home, and set up income streams to cover their routine expenses. They were living life well and had few financial worries. They even traveled a little to different places around the world for fun and for mission trips. And they traveled a lot around the country to see their kids. After their first grandchild arrived, their travel back to Illinois became much more frequent. Even with all their travel expenses, their probability score remained high (around 90%), and they felt confident in their finances.

As time went by, however, George and Linda longed to be closer to family and their grandson. But that meant an unplanned move, more money for a home, a more expensive mortgage based on higher interest rates, and higher property taxes. Naturally, they felt uncertain and thought maybe they shouldn't do it as the costs kept adding up. We re-ran their analysis with the new scenario, and instead of 90%, we got projections around 70%.

Who wants a 70%? If you're thinking about this score like letter grades, that would mean they have a C- or a D+. But here's the thing... we're not trying to get 100% on this exam. Yes, each percentage point of probability means more successful missions, i.e., your rocket has enough fuel to make it to its intended target (which is your death :)), and it also delivers $1 or more of cargo.

Understand, though, that each percentage point you fall short of 100% doesn't mean your rocket blows up. If your probability score is 70%, that means 70% of the time, you will get where you're going. The other 30% of simulations mean that if you keep burning fuel by flying the rocket at the same speed (spending the same projected amounts each year) and carrying the same weight (e.g., a second home or a boat), you wouldn't have enough fuel to get where you're going. But 70% of the time, you would!

I call the 30% of these simulations "adjustment periods" rather than "failures." They are inflection points when your probability dips low enough that you should probably consider slowing down (spending less) or dumping some weight (selling the second home or downsizing your primary home).

In essence, you have one more safety net. Unlike space travel, where you have very few destinations, your intentional retirement can include stops in many new places if your plan needs to adjust!

When working with clients at the point of retirement transition, because of all these variables, we are guiding them toward an ideal probability score of 75-90%. This score means you're using your money well to spend and give along the way, have a strong probability that there will not only be enough (but likely some left over), and you're accepting enough ups and downs in the market to give your investments the opportunity to grow.

George's and Linda's new score would dip below the confidence zone if they made the move and built the home they wanted in Illinois. But they'd be close to their grandson and have the new lifestyle they wanted. As a result of their thoughtful consideration, they made an intentional and confident decision to change their plan. We now have contingencies in place for how to adjust their future spending if it ever comes to that. Odds are, it won't, and in the meantime, they are enjoying life and couldn't be happier that they made the change!

This story illustrates the power of using projections to make informed and intentional decisions. On one end of the Monte Carlo projection spectrum, your probability may dip so low that it's critical to adjust, spend less, or save more. At the other end, scores sometimes are well above 90%, and trend even higher. If that's the case for you, then as good as it may make you feel to see 99%, your high probability means that you are likely under-utilizing your assets and could spend more, give more, or shift them to have more growth potential by taking on more risk.

Decisions, Decisions...

Al is a wonderful, caring man who values family, hard work, and preserving his finances to take care of his son, who faces an uncertain economic future due to some special needs. Al lost his wife just before their retirement, and he has struggled to make decisions without his lifelong partner to help him prioritize. Even more than all the financial changes he's faced since her death, this loss of a decision-making partner has probably been the biggest issue for his financial future.

Shortly after his wife died, Al suffered a work-related injury to his hand that prevented him from being able to continue working. It was an unnerving time for him and his finances, but our company has helped people through similar situations on countless occasions. Al and I went through the first two steps of our process— Organize and Prioritize—and we came up with his probability score. Prior to this planning process, Al chose not to do much extra or spend anything over his budget because he wondered if he had enough. What if he could never work again? Would there be enough to last for his lifetime? What if he died too soon or lived too long? How could he provide for his son?

Any guess as to what score we came up with when we ran Al's Monte Carlo simulation? It was 99%! Establishing this level of confidence allowed Al and me to refocus our conversation on how to accomplish his goals rather than worrying about if he could do it.

There are many people, perhaps even you, who would likely also score a 99%, even though they worry about the same things Al did: Living too long, declines in net worth, spending too much, experiencing market losses, and leaving enough for family. Perhaps you even worry as much as Al did. You might feel that 99% isn't good enough. Well, guess what? You can't score 100% in a Monte Carlo simulation, so let's move beyond some of that worry.

The foundational first step is to calculate your score, and regardless of what score you get (if it soars at 91%+, or lands in the "confidence zone" between 75-90%, or if it falls much lower than you'd hoped), we all have work to do. Because everything to this point just tells us *IF* your plan is probable, it doesn't yet tell us how to do it!

"How do I get money into my checking account when my paycheck stops?"

This is one of the most common practical/logistical questions people ask us when we first meet. It's a little scary if you think about it. For the last 20, 30, or 40-plus years, you've exchanged your labor, skills, and expertise for a paycheck. Perhaps it showed up every two weeks, 2x/month, or once a month. Perhaps it was a fixed amount, or maybe it varied check-to-check based on your performance at work. No matter the details, you built your living and spending patterns around that paycheck. Yet when you retire, that paycheck stops! So, how do we replace it?

Popular song lyrics in the late 90s sung by Montell Jordan go, "This is how we do it." When he proclaimed that, everyone tuned in to listen. Unfortunately, I don't have anything quite as simple or catchy as that song to help you think about how to get income in retirement. But author and speaker Tom Hegna certainly does. His book, titled *Paychecks and Playchecks* outlines a process for how he would recommend creating income. I encourage you to buy and read that book! In short, Tom Hegna advocates for lining up income sources that pay consistently to you so you can cover your routine expenses. Sound familiar?

Step three of our Retire Intentionally process is *Strategize*. Evaluating multiple strategies is crucial to all aspects of a financial plan, but it is most critical to understand and consider the pros/cons of a variety of strategies when you're choosing how to create your paychecks.

The first thing I hope you latch on to is this fact…
there is not one right way to do it. Read a lot. Learn a
lot. Partner with an advisor. Ask around. When you
do, please remember that if someone is telling you
they know the *RIGHT* way or that someone else's way
is the *WRONG* way, then you're likely not getting the
whole story.

One of the buzzwords in the financial industry
is "fiduciary." A fiduciary's role is to be a caretaker/
coach/guide/advisor who puts others' interests
ahead of their own. My business partner, Corey, and
I have been fiduciaries since the early 2000s when
we earned our CFP® designations and committed to
that fiduciary standard. Our company's most recent
partner, Jacob, is also a CFP® and a fiduciary. We
think putting others' interests first is a good way to live
life, and as it turns out, it's been a great way to build
a business.

Regulatory changes over the last few years have
made it so most advisors in the financial industry
must now commit to the fiduciary standard. This is
great in many ways, but it's also caused confusion.
It's confusing because some groups of people
have started to market themselves as fiduciaries
solely because they charge fees for their advice or
investment management rather than commissions.
In my opinion, the way a person makes their living
or is compensated for services does not determine
if they are a fiduciary. Commissions or fees don't

determine if you are or are not working with a fiduciary.

I believe that a fiduciary should equip you, teach you, empower you, and advise you about all your choices.

If your advisor can't offer you multiple choices, it creates conflicts of interest. If there is a lack of transparency on this issue of "choice" or a general disregard or dismissal of alternative options, it may mean that you are NOT working with a fiduciary, regardless of what their card says.

This fiduciary relationship is critical when you start selecting how to create your paychecks in retirement because there are lots of ways to do it. None are necessarily right or wrong, and each has its pros and cons, but I think all should be considered and discussed with your planning partner. In general, there are several broad categories that we try to help clients understand when it comes to creating their paychecks.

Paycheck Categories

1. **Guaranteed**[5] lifetime income (Social Security, pensions, and lifetime annuities).
2. **Reliable** lifetime income (rental income, business income, dividends, and interest).
3. **Withdrawal** income (selling assets or distributing principal).

I'll go into detail on each category in the pages that follow, but please keep in mind I am not recommending any specific strategy for you. Each of these options has drawbacks and negative components. Each has positive attributes and compelling features. More than likely, you've already formed opinions about which option is good or bad because we're often conditioned to think binary— that one is right, and one is wrong. I'm asking you to set those pre-conceived notions aside and be open-minded as you read the next story. As always, I'm not telling you what will work for you, and I'm certainly not saying the choices one couple made are right for everyone. I'm just sharing an example of how they found more confidence regarding HOW to spend, give, and live in retirement.

---

[5] An implied guarantee is only as good as the issuing body, whether the government, insurance agency, or a pension fund. Please carefully review any income sources from these categories to ensure you understand the risks.

Opposites Attract

Calvin and Katie are an incredibly complementary match. She likes to know every detail and wants to fact-check each part of their financial situation. He likes to make money and spend money. Thankfully, they both liked to save, and they prepared well for retirement. We have worked together for years and have made choices about Social Security (she started her smaller benefit earlier, and he deferred his larger benefit until age 70), made decisions on his pension (including lifetime spousal benefits), and segmented assets to avoid risk on some investments while positioning others for long-term growth. We planned to use interest and dividends from parts of their portfolio and sell from the principal of other parts when it was an opportune time.

In our company, we refer to this as diversifying risk. I introduced this topic previously and now would like to elaborate; we segment parts of a portfolio through the following methods:

- Avoiding risk on parts of the portfolio by using cash and fixed assets.
- Absorbing risk with other parts of the portfolio by blending bonds and stocks, as well as index funds and mutual funds.
- Accepting risk by picking long-term, low-cost options that can track markets when we're confident that we don't *have* to sell them for regular income.

- Transferring risk to protect against negative circumstances that could impact your plan (which was especially important in this couple's situation).

Calvin and Katie weren't quite content with their plan because they worried about having consistent income to cover all their routine expenses, and they wanted to make sure that the income would last as long as they did. Katie's family, especially, has a history of longevity, and she was in great health. Despite her aversion to the words "annuity" and "life insurance" and her negative view about the "extremely high fees" on "variable annuities," they were open to learning about these tools.

We reviewed all the pros and cons of different types of life insurance and annuities as we built their retirement income and inheritance plan. To them, it was important to not only make sure that Katie had income for her long life, but they also wanted to protect her if Calvin died at a young age (due to some health issues they were monitoring). Regardless of their own mortality or longevity, they wanted to pass on money to their only child, a daughter, to increase her financial security.

After many discussions, meetings, and adjustments over several years, their plan now includes two annuities: A single, lifetime annuity in Katie's name that provides her income as long as she lives and a variable annuity in Calvin's name that provides them income, market potential, and a death benefit guarantee that gives Katie, or their daughter, a lump sum if Calvin dies first.

They also pay significant amounts each year for second-to-die life insurance that pays out a designated inheritance to their daughter as a tax-free lump sum when they've both passed away. There are obviously drawbacks and tradeoffs to each of the tools they're using, but they value the benefits and how these tools fit with the rest of their stocks, index funds, and mutual funds.

When we were recently reviewing their plan, I reminded them about some of the tradeoffs and how they've intentionally brought their probability to a lower number in their Monte Carlo simulations (because they're traveling more, giving more, and paying into the life insurance for the inheritance). Calvin responded with this: "Yeah, but even if we run out, we can still live on ncome for the rest of our lives."

For them, the certainty that comes with having the income and inheritance plans in place gives them more confidence to help their daughter now, give very generously (they were audited for "giving too much" several times throughout their working years), and, of course, have a lot of fun spending it. Their plan has also given them the confidence to hold investments when the market drops and be opportunistic to invest more when it's down. It allows them to focus on living well rather than worrying about running out.

Is Calvin and Katie's strategy for creating income and having discretionary money the right strategy for you? Maybe not. To be right implies that there's another strategy that's wrong. Calvin and Katie have one that works for them. It is intentional, and it gives them the confidence to spend and give how they want.

Retire Intentionally Exercise

Before you go any further, please visit www.retire-intentionally.com to create a draft of your Monte Carlo simulation. You just might be surprised how you score!

Scan for end of chapter worksheets or visit Retire-Intentionally.com

Chapter 6
Maximize Your Money

"When money realizes it's in good hands, it
wants to stay and multiply in those hands."
~Idowu Koyenikan

L et's dive a little deeper into what gives Calvin and Katie the confidence that they have gained through the years and explore how their story might help you on your journey to retire intentionally. In an earlier chapter, I covered how you can calculate your routine expenses by adding up credits, debits, and cash.

I'd like for you to now add up your recurring income by totaling the deposits that you can count on each month for the rest of your life.

As a reminder, here are the categories that retirement income typically falls within.

Retirement Income Categories

1. Guaranteed lifetime income (Social Security, pensions, and lifetime annuities).
2. Reliable lifetime income (rental income, business income, dividends, and interest).
3. Withdrawal income (selling assets or distributing principal).

Guaranteed lifetime income may seem ideal, but it is often the least flexible. Social Security, pensions, and lifetime annuity income are typically the main sources most people live on. I'm not going to go into much detail on annuities and pensions because not everyone has or needs those, but nearly everyone has Social Security as their baseline recurring income, so I do want to cover a few key points.

Here are the basics: You've earned income throughout your life and with each paycheck, Social Security taxes have been assessed and set aside in a massive trust fund that is run by the Social Security Administration. You can generally begin to receive your payments at 62, and you can defer distribution until age 70. Full-retirement-age (FRA) is probably around age 67 (this adjusts based on your birth year). Once you've hit your FRA, you can collect your full Social Security payment; it will be lower if you take it earlier and higher if you wait longer, up until the maximum age of 70. Once you select your age to begin payments, your income is likely set (there will be the potential for cost-of-living adjustments, but your income likely won't change again because of your age). If you or your spouse didn't have enough credits to earn an individual benefit, you/they may qualify for a spousal benefit, which is roughly half the primary earner's benefit.

Generally, most couples have two Social Security payments each month for as long as they live. When the first person dies, the surviving spouse keeps the larger of the two payments for the rest of their life. Because of this spousal benefit, it is incredibly important to consider two major things when making your decisions:

1. Longevity
2. Percentage of income/resources

The longer you are likely to live, the more you are likely to receive in total lifetime benefits by deferring the age at which you start your Social Security payments. You can and should get projections of your individual benefits from SSA.gov and then run a "break-even" analysis so you understand the math. Oftentimes, the break-even occurs in your early eighties. This process compares starting your benefit early (with a lower payment) to deferring it and taking it at a later age (with a higher payment). It determines an inflection point (usually in your early eighties) where you are likely to get more, in total, out of the Social Security system because you waited longer, and then each additional month you live gives you more money.

But that only tells part of the story...

If Social Security makes up a high percentage of your income and potential income (from assets), then it's probably important to defer your payment as long as possible so you have more money later. If you have other significant assets or income, however, there are many reasons to consider taking it sooner. I'll list just a few reasons to take earlier and later and then share stories of intentional retirement decisions.

Show Me the Money (take it now):

- **The Social Security Trust Fund Is Underfunded**: Recent studies are projecting 2033 as a year when benefits could drop.

- **You Can't Take It with You**: Of course, you can't take any of your money with you when you die, but you can leave other assets and investments to your beneficiaries. You cannot leave your Social Security retirement benefits to your children. Only your spouse can be a beneficiary of your Social Security payment (if it's higher than theirs), meaning if you die young, your family can't benefit from all that you've paid into the trust fund.

- **Paychecks Are Easy to Spend**: For many retirees, it is emotionally challenging to "spend down" their assets. Yet, when money is deposited in your checking account from Social Security, it's likely easier, mentally and emotionally, to spend those dollars than it is to withdraw extra from your savings.

- **Taxation**: You know your current tax rate and may think it's better to pay a lower rate now than a potentially higher rate later.

- **Lack of Longevity**: You're concerned that you and/or your spouse won't live long enough to reap the benefits of deferring, so enjoy it now.

Hold, Please (defer it):

- **Longevity**: If you are a healthy couple at 65, most actuarial projections will show that at least one of you will live until your early nineties. That's a lot of years to get a bigger paycheck by waiting to start.

- **Taxation**: The lower your total income, the lower your percentage of Social Security that gets taxed. So, if you can defer your Social Security income until later, it gives you opportunities to relocate your money between the ages of 62-70 across the tax efficiency spreadsheet. This could mean spending IRA money first, converting IRAs to ROTH, or using other re-positioning strategies that will lower future income. If you have a reduced future income, you can potentially have a lot less of your Social Security benefits exposed to taxation.

- **Recurring Income**: As previously mentioned, Social Security is a stable, consistent paycheck. If you can defer your benefits to the point where Social Security plus other recurring income covers most of your routine expenses, then you'll have more confidence that you'll always have enough income for a normal life. This confidence often provides the boost for people to spend or give more from other investments at younger ages because they have enough lifetime income.

Planning for a Potential Inheritance... or Not

Marc and Maryjo have a strong and secure retirement plan and an investment portfolio that has allowed them to retire young in their early sixties. They have launched their kids through college and into young adulthood, and they now enjoy traveling on their own and with their grown children. Through the years, they have given generously to church and charities while saving and investing aggressively. They have been fortunate to receive some financial gifts from their parents along the way and now choose to help their kids in a similar fashion as their next generation starts families.

We've loaded their routine expenses, wants, and wishes into their financial plan, and their probability score is in the confidence zone (75-90%). Marc and Maryjo also have the awareness that they will likely receive an inheritance in the future, and I've counseled them that there's a difference between "awareness" and "reliance" when it comes to a potential inheritance. Inheritances can be tough to discuss for many reasons, and one of the ways that many people may deflect that discomfort is to say things like "I don't even want it!"

or *"I just hope my parents spend and enjoy it instead of worrying about giving it to me!"*

Guess what? A theoretical inheritance, meaning one that *might* come to you someday, isn't about YOU and what you want. It's what the other generation wants, and it's about what they value in their money. If they've been frugal their entire life, they likely don't have any desire to spend it the way you may want them to or the way you might want to. And if they want to give you money, then maybe ask them "why" that's important to them, rather than telling them how they should use their money.

If you're fortunate enough to receive an inheritance someday, then you can decide if you do or don't want it, and you can decide how to spend, save, give, and enjoy that money. Until that time, I would suggest you factor in an awareness of that possible inheritance into your financial plan. I would also caution against relying on that possible inheritance to make too many decisions early on.

For Marc and Maryjo, this meant that years ago, we put a potential placeholder in their plan. We ran one version of their plan with it, showing how the plan would improve if they received it, and we ran another with the inheritance placeholder excluded.

We still don't count on the money as being part of their plan, but as the years have gone by, the awareness has increased that it's now more likely that they'll receive something. This has caused us to change our approach to Social Security. Instead of deferring Marc's benefits all the way until he reaches 70, he and Maryjo have decided to take it sooner. Doing so provides them with more confidence to spend now—due to a higher monthly income—and allows them to invest their other funds more aggressively (which aligns with their risk tolerance).

Marc and Maryjo are aware that by taking their Social Security earlier, they have created some additional risk. If there is a triple whammy (that's my very technical financial term for three unlikely things happening at the same time), then their plan is negatively impacted by their decision. In this case, their triple whammy would be longevity (that they would both live until 100), under-performing investments, and receiving no inheritance. If one or two of these events occur, their plan still works, but if all three happen, then they may need to slow their spending and shift their giving to later in retirement.

The Likely Longevity Couple

Mike and Rhea have a different approach to their decision-making but have agreed to start their benefits much earlier than age 70. Their financial plan is well-diversified both in terms of allocation and location, and they have a very high probability of success when running their Monte Carlo analysis.

Mike loves a good spreadsheet to run quantitative analyses, and he knows the math very well for his Social Security situation. They are in good health and have a strong probability of living well past their break-even ages, which would cause many people to defer. Yet, Mike wanted their money now. It allows them to spend and invest with more confidence, and it gives them a chance to make more by investing it than they would by deferring it. Most importantly, once they get a payment, it's theirs. There is no longer a possibility that the government can tax it differently, reduce it because of a depleting Social Security trust fund, or offset it because of their assets and income.

Your decision about how to create income and when to take Social Security is personal. It can't be decided by a book or article or by doing what your friend does.

I encourage you to: Learn it. Know it. Model it. And ultimately make an intentional decision that aligns your money with your priorities and values. Remember, as well, that this is likely only a part of your retirement spending plan.

Now, let's focus on some other common ways that people create recurring income to cover their routine expenses:

- Interest and Dividends
- Business/Rental Income
- Selling Assets (stocks/funds)
- Annuities
- Pensions

Before I go into brief descriptions and options for each category, it's important to reinforce why these options will matter to you.

Welcome to Adulthood

When I was 23, fresh out of college and new to my career, I went on the first vacation of my adult life. A group of friends and I went to the Bahamas over the New Year's holiday. It was an incredible getaway filled with fun and adventures. It also cost a lot of money! But for the first time in my life, I wasn't stressed about spending my money or charging purchases on my debit/credit cards.

As the days wore on, I knew I was reaching my "budget" for the trip and even quickly passing it, but I had the confidence to keep enjoying myself.

This confidence replaced many prior feelings of anxiety about spending because I had something new in my life... a regular paycheck! My paycheck was a whopping $2,000 per month at the beginning of 2002, but it was enough for me to pay all my normal bills, plus I had the potential to make more.

Perhaps you've already traveled to start your retirement, or you soon will. Many people plan a big trip to mark this transition, and I want you to have the confidence to spend money and enjoy it if you do something similar. Part of the confidence to do so comes from the assurance that you can return home from this trip (and a lot of future trips) and know that you'll have a "paycheck" to keep paying your normal bills.

I want you to have a retirement like that. One that allows you to go have fun spending and giving. I want you to know that every month, you can afford the basics again. Tom Hegna would say this happens when you have your paychecks covered! Here are some ways that people create their paychecks:

- **Interest and Dividends**: This is one of the most basic categories. In its simplest form, interest might occur when you deposit your money in a bank account (or buy a bond or CD), which secures your principal and permits you to collect interest. For the past 15-20 years, this has been a challenging strategy because interest rates were so low. Now, with short-term interest rates around 5%, it's a much more enjoyable option because your $500,000 could provide you interest of

$25,000/year or just over $2,000/month if you take it as a "paycheck."

Dividends are a similar concept, but unlike interest being paid on a fixed asset, dividends are a return of profit from a company/investment, and the underlying investment will likely change in value on a daily or regular basis. Dividend rates are generally lower than interest rates but also provide the opportunity for your underlying investment to appreciate.

- **Annuities**: We're moving from one of the most basic categories to the most complex. Simplified, an annuity is a contract where you exchange a lump sum of money for one of two benefits: *Growth potential/deferred income or immediate income.* There are many reasons to consider deferred annuities as part of your plan, and there are many reasons to avoid them. This book is not focused on whether you should or shouldn't use them, but I urge you to think about this: If your "advisor" says they are terrible and they don't/can't offer them, I'd be curious about why you don't have the choice. Conversely, if your "advisor" says they are amazing, and that's all they use/can offer, I'd be curious as to why you don't have more choices.

For the purposes of this section, we'll focus on the *income* aspect of annuities. There are many ways to structure benefits (fixed periods, lifetime benefits, percentage-based withdrawals, for example), and none of them are inherently right/wrong. They are just ways you can structure your investments to pay you income, and that is the goal—creating recurring income that covers routine expenses. For this reason, they should certainly be evaluated as a tool.

- **Business/Rental Income**: Like dividends, this category relies on the performance of an underlying company or rental property to produce a profit and ultimately pay out part of that profit on a regular basis. Unlike dividends from stock market investments, this income is ideal because it usually provides an uncorrelated return (it won't necessarily go up or down directly with the stock market). The main drawback is less marketability, meaning you can't easily sell your investment right away to get the funds back if you want them.

- **Pensions**: Ahhh… the good ol' days! Most people do not have this option, but those who do can sit pretty. A pension is basically a retirement benefit guaranteed by an organization, company, or government agency that pays you a consistent monthly paycheck throughout your retirement. If this is part of your plan, carefully evaluate the pros and cons of lump sum payments compared to lifetime payments, and understand all your options for single or joint life payments. Then, enjoy the paycheck! If you can't include this in your plan, focus on the three aforementioned categories, as well as the following:

- **Consistent Selling**: We have already covered some of the pros and cons of this strategy; to reiterate, it essentially means picking an investment and selling it at a good time and for a good price. It works well if you always have good timing and a good price! It's less than ideal when prices drop, and your timing is forced on you due to an unexpected event or simply because you need your next paycheck and have to sell.

We have helped clients make the retirement transition through the bursting of the tech bubble ('00-'02), the Great Recession/ the Global Financial Crisis ('07-'09), and countless other crazy happenings over the last 15 years: (Brexit, government stalemates, volatile interest rates, COVID, and much more). Nobody that we've worked with as an "engaged partner" has gone back to work because they've had to. They've been able to rely on their paycheck strategies for recurring income to cover their routine expenses and have waited for better timing and pricing to sell their other investments for "playchecks."

Playchecks

Allow me to reference, once again, Tom Hegna's research and perspectives for the title of this next section because, honestly, paychecks are boring. We designed that part of a plan to cover the basics of life. But intentional retirements are about so much more than the basics.

Your retirement will provide more time to play, and you probably could use some money to do it. There will also be projects to do, people and organizations to help, and unexpected circumstances to deal with. Tom Hegna refers to the money to cover these elements as "playchecks." During your working years, you have likely paid for these irregular expenses from sources such as emergency funds, bonuses, or stock distributions. In retirement, however, there are no more bonuses or stock grants from your company. Your entire net worth is now your "emergency fund," which can be both freeing and paralyzing.

How are you supposed to decide how much you can spend, and just as importantly, how are you supposed to pick the most efficient place to take it from?

The DIYs

Jordan and Jess are people I have met with, but they are not clients. They are do-it-yourselfers who have accumulated more than enough for retirement.

According to the Millionaire Next Door book, they are PAWs. They have built up a significant cash reserve and feel great about it, especially since their $300,000 in money market funds is generating about $15,000/ year of interest. They have over $1,000,000 in IRAs, $200,000 in mutual funds and stocks in a brokerage account, and $100,000 in ROTH IRAs. They receive about $50,000 in Social Security benefits each year and would like to spend $80,000/year on basic expenses, meaning they need about $30,000 extra. Jordan's plan was to withdraw $30,000/year from his cash reserves and keep deferring his IRA until he is forced to take required minimum distributions (RMDs) at age 73. He hates paying taxes and is excited about the plan he created because he will initially have no federal income taxes.

Their basic plan is on track, and their potential playchecks would be $10,000/year for travel and $8,000/year for charitable giving. They also plan on buying a new car approximately every five years. I asked how they would cover these extras, and Jordan responded that they would spend the cash, so there are "No taxes!"

Although the numbers vary across our client base, Jordan's and Jess' situation is quite common and his initial approach is also quite popular. We try to expand that approach in the fourth part of our planning process as we seek to *Maximize* the impact of people's money. Partly, this comes through increasing efficiency by minimizing unnecessary taxes, risk, and fees. Additionally, it comes from exploring creative ways to use all the tools on the tax-efficiency checklist, as well as generosity tools like donor-advised funds and qualified charitable distributions, and estate planning concepts like lifetime gifting, life insurance, and trusts.

We'll cover more of those creative concepts in the third section of the book, but let's first finish Jordan's and Jess' story to better understand how they planned to get their playchecks. Perhaps you share the same perspective that Jordan does on taxes, and you'd like to pay as little as possible, too. Most people I've met want to minimize taxes, and if that's you, then I invite you to change your perspective— start thinking about your lifelong tax burden, not just how to write a smaller check to the IRS this year.

Let me ask you: Do you think tax rates will be lower now or in the future?

We could debate federal tax rates all day long, but it's not worth our time. The truth is that none of us truly know what will happen, but you're entitled to your guess. My guess is that, in general, they likely won't be lower in the years to come. Although I can't predict the future for our country's taxes, I can more closely predict the future for you if you're a couple filing jointly now. If you're currently married, filing jointly, then your personal tax burden is likely to go up when one of you passes away. This phenomenon is illustrated by the tax chart, below, showing how more income is subjected to higher marginal rates after a death that changes tax-filer status from joint to single. You can also access it at www.intentgen.com/resources in the 2024 Financial Planning Guide.

I also know two other facts about income taxes that haven't changed in recent history: We have a marginal tax bracket system (that means your tax rate goes up as you earn/withdraw more), and we have a standard deduction (that means you don't have to pay tax on all your income). Thus, even if rates do go up in the future, there is still likely to be a low bracket where you can draw out some of your money without paying any tax, and there will probably be room to withdraw some additional funds at a very low bracket.

By taking primarily from their cash reserves and Social Security, Jordan and Jess weren't creating enough adjusted gross income (AGI) to use up their standard deduction (currently about $30,000 for joint filers 65-plus). This means that they could have withdrawn spending money from their IRAs or converted their IRAs to ROTH IRAs without paying any income tax.

I'm not an accountant and can't give you tax advice, but I would suggest that you learn about standard deductions, partial taxation of Social Security benefits (based on other income), and that you run tax simulations or work with an accountant to see if you can get some of your playchecks without taxation, or at least, minimal taxation.

Jordan and Jess didn't want to learn about these factors and are now unintentionally and unnecessarily rolling the dice on tax rates. By deferring all their IRAs, they're increasing their future required minimum distributions (RMDs) and will have to pay tax on them at potentially higher marginal tax rates and single tax filer rates. This also means that their income will be higher in the future, and they may be unnecessarily exposed to increased Medicare premiums.

None of this information persuaded this couple to think differently, so I brought up perhaps the most significant tax-related maximization opportunity that applied to them—the 0% cap gains rate for long-term capital gains that are recognized when your income is in the 12% ordinary income bracket. These DIYers were dismissive because they said it sounded confusing, they didn't want to pay an accountant to figure it out, plus they really liked their stock that had appreciated so much. There was not a lot I could do to help at that point, especially since they weren't willing to listen to the fact that they could sell some of their stock, pay no federal capital gains taxes, and then immediately repurchase it.

"What about the 'wash sale rule" *for selling stocks and repurchasing them?" Jordan asked. I tried to explain that the rule only applied to losses and that it would be ideal for them to sell stocks for their playchecks and recognize gains at a 0% rate. But they had their plan, and they wanted to stick to it.*

If all this feels a little complex to you, that's okay... it should! I'll quickly summarize this section by saying that you likely could benefit from partnering with a proactive accountant and a financial advisor who understands lifetime tax perspectives. Many people I encounter initially judge the success of a tax year on whether they got a refund.

I want you to judge the success of your financial situation on your lifetime impact—and I want to help you maximize your impact by looking at a lifetime of tax returns.

Unfortunately, Jordan was stubborn and didn't want to hear it. After all, he and Jess were millionaires who had invested in a low-cost, diversified portfolio. They had enough money for retirement, and they had done it all themselves.

---

* The wash sale rule prevents a taxpayer from selling an investment for a loss, to reduce their tax bill and then repurchasing the same investment within 30 days. If repurchased within 30 days, the prior loss is "washed away" and doesn't count for that time period. Please consult a tax advisor or tax software program for more detail.

For the most part, I applaud them. Jordan and Jess managed the accumulation phase of their life quite well, and they created a comfortable retirement. But they were a long way from maximizing the distribution phase of their lifetime. As it turned out, they were so focused on accumulating money and seeing their net worth go up that regardless of the withdrawal strategy, they couldn't even allow themselves to take out money for playchecks. I wish they would have given me the opportunity to partner with them and not just so we had another client. I wish that we could have worked together so that they could have given themselves permission to use their money for themselves and others.

I tried again years later to partner with them. At this next meeting, they were proud of their progress— their net worth had grown, and their balance sheet was bigger—but they had not used very much money to give and live. They were not tracking a "joy" or "giving" column on their net worth statement and were still filled with worry.

To me, the sad part is not just their lack of maximization, even though that likely would have amounted to a difference measured in the tens of thousands of dollars throughout their lifetime. Although that's real money, those extra dollars likely won't change their life. The missed opportunity is more significant— it's that they couldn't embrace the importance of intentionality and generosity in their retirement planning. They focused on numbers and not on impact. The potential that stems from our planning process— when we partner with people to *Organize, Prioritize, Strategize, and Maximize*— is often measured in terms of joy, experiences, and impact, which is what we strive to help people maximize the most.

Jordan and Jess defined their progress by the size of their net worth number. How will you define your progress throughout your intentional retirement?

Retire Intentionally Exercise

To help you better understand the ins and outs of IRMAA and how they can affect you, I have included a chart at www.retire-intentionally.com.

Scan for end of chapter worksheets or visit Retire-Intentionally.com

Net Impact

The Depth of Net Impact

"A life is not important except in the impact it has on other lives."
~Jackie Robinson

When you choose to be kind to someone, it is typically easy to identify the impact but often hard to quantify the depth of that impact.

For instance, when you are nice to someone, you're likely aware that it made them feel good because of how they responded, with a smile or "thank you." In turn, your kindness might produce many positive ripple effects if the recipient was then nicer to others throughout that day.

But how can you really measure the impact of kindness or encouragement?

Some other actions have positive impacts that are more easily calculated. If you help a student, colleague, or family member learn a skill or solve a problem, they not only experience immediate progress, but you might also be able to measure that impact by tracking future outcomes—e.g., learning the skill led to more money, fewer expenses, more success, etc.

A third type of impact is less direct and more long-term in nature. When you plant a tree, give money to a charity, or invest in your grandchildren's education, the true impact and outcomes may not be evident for decades. In this instance, it's often more important to focus on the inputs rather than the outcomes. And it's from this long-term perspective that I'd like to introduce to you the last part of your intentional retirement plan: Net Impact.

Remember, your intentional retirement begins with a net worth mindset and then shifts to a net income strategy. If you can use your income strategies to support your lifestyle, then you start to block out the worry and unlock the impact of your entire worth—your skills, your time, and your money. Amazing opportunities lie ahead when you begin to clarify the impact and experiences you want to create for yourself, your family, and others.

In short...your net impact will be calculated by defining and adding:

Income + Experiences + Purpose And, not in that order...

Purpose is ultimately at the core of who you are, and in my opinion and that of David (referenced in a prior story), it should be the first thing that you think about in retirement.

Who are you? (What are your most important values, character traits, and the roles you fill? (E.g., parent, friend, grandparent, athlete, leader, volunteer...)

What do you value and enjoy? (What are your hobbies, interests, activities, and skills?)

How will you spend your time and money?

Who are the people and places that matter to you? (E.g., family, friends, church, teams, clubs, non-profit organizations.)

Because it's hard for most people to think so profoundly or existentially, our planning process starts with income (cash flow). The previous chapters should have provided a pathway to increase your confidence that your expenses can be covered for your normal life. Our planning partnerships are designed to do this, as well, and I invite you to engage us if you'd like a partner.

With this increased confidence in cash flow, it becomes easier to think about what's next. Envisioning and planning out experiences are the next steps, and I encourage you now to dream about the experiences you want during your retirement:

Who are you with? (Family, friends, yourself?)

Where are you? (Enjoying international tours or national parks? Are you rustic or fancy? In a campground or at a luxury resort?)

What are you doing? (Relaxing? Reveling in adventures? Are you learning? Serving?)

When you start to create the mental picture of these experiences, we can begin to attach price tags and placeholders to them. Your plan might include possible distributions for weddings, family trips, house projects, or anything else that made your list. Knowing this, we can then model it in a Monte Carlo simulation and see if you have enough.

If you have special goals, desires, and plans for your retirement, I suggest that you coordinate a team (comprised of family members, an advisor, and specialists) to help you clarify your retirement income, experiences, and purpose.

Concentrating on these areas of special importance in your retirement plan will allow you to focus on your net impact.

Here is the final formula:

Net Worth + Net Income = Net Impact

Expand and written slightly differently, you could think of it this way:

Assets + Income – Liabilities – Expenses – Taxes = Net Impact

We'll unpack this formula in the last few chapters, starting first with defining your experiences as I've described below. We'll then focus on maximizing your money and charitable impact and close with some final concepts pertaining to purpose.

1. **There Is Always a Bigger Boat.** Although it is exciting to think about and plan for doing more, this chapter will also help you discover ways to find joy in the ordinary. Your Intentional Retirement can strike a balance of contentment and achievement.

2. **Give It Away, Give It Away, Give It Away Now.** If you are in a position of financial strength, I want to help you consider the positive impacts and influences you can have on the people and places you care about. Is there more you could be doing now rather than worrying about what ifs that could happen later? And finally, could it be that you actually receive when you give?

3. **To Be(queath) or Not to Be(queath).** Many want to leave an inheritance to people and places they care about. This chapter will help you reexamine how to do that and how much you may want to prioritize and give to your financial legacy.

After all, this is about you... your money, your timing, and your purpose. You may want to see and experience the immediate impact, or you may choose to invest in a long-term impact that will have ripple effects for generations.

Chapter 7
There Is Always a Bigger Boat

"The only limit to your impact is your imagination
and commitment"
~Tony Robbins

Remember the recent story about Jordan and Jess? They focused so much on growing their net worth that they had trouble using the money for experiences along the way. There is also an opposite end of the spectrum...

When the Rug Is Ripped out from Under You

Joyce lost her husband just before her retirement. After years of careful accumulation planning, she felt she had a thoughtful strategy for income that would cover her basic expenses for her lifetime. Losing her husband changed things in so many ways, but revisions to her financial plan rebuilt her confidence, and she was excited to find there was also going to be enough money for experiences and impact.

Joyce has prioritized her family and wants to help her grown children with new homes and paying for her grandkids' educations. Those are amazing ways to prioritize using one's money, but she has paired those goals with one other goal that will wreak havoc on her plan: A lake home that could be used for family gatherings. Although the cost of this home fit well into her plan, Joyce made some inaccurate assumptions about how her family might help pay for things in the future. She focused on the experiences but failed to account for the "obligations" that come with her lake home: Insurance, boat, docks, maintenance, plus non-stop expenditures to host gatherings. And the kids didn't or couldn't help as much as Joyce had hoped, resulting in "playcheck" disbursements that became too frequent and too large, and in turn, began to draw down her reserves too quickly.

You can come to your own conclusions about Joyce's story. It was her fault for spending too recklessly. It was my fault for not keeping her aware of her downward trajectory and cautioning her to slow down (which I did on a consistent basis). Some may applaud Joyce for "enjoying it now" and using it while she is younger and can have fun at the lake. Still others will shame Joyce's kids for taking advantage of their mom by accepting gifts as adults and not helping more with expenses.

In many ways, each perspective is fair and has some validity. But none of us has the right to judge… because this is Joyce's story and her experience. I share her story because I think what her plan lacked was intentionality. Too frequently, she was making these spur-of-the-moment decisions that never seemed too big by themselves: $5,000 for a project, $10,000 for education, $20,000 for the boat, and $3,000 for new appliances. Over time, they added up to more than $100,000, and each time they hit, they drove up tax brackets and Medicare costs. And then, the insurance premiums increased, the fuel bills climbed, there were repairs on the house and boat, and the sporadic educational support turned into regular payments.

Joyce's *experiences* turned into *obligations*. We can use what she went through to understand the difference between the two—a critical distinction when it comes to your intentional retirement. Here's how I define the difference between them from a financial and retirement planning perspective: *Experiences* are one-time events that use a specific amount of money in a finite period, e.g., renting a lake home for a week with your family, taking a cruise with friends, or redoing your back patio. *Obligations* are major events that use a specific amount of money and lead to additional amounts of money for an extended timeframe, e.g., buying a lake home, purchasing a boat, joining a country club, or building a pool. While each of these obligations provides incredible ongoing experiences, they also have additional fixed and variable costs that extend as long as you have them in your life.

In the middle of the spectrum, between Joyce's story of obligations that led to financial problems and Jordan's and Jess' story of no experiences that led to a ballooning net worth, is an intentional middle-ground, filled with experiences, obligations, and contentment.

What do you think of when you read the word "experiences?" Many people gravitate toward travel and vacation. Others imagine time at home. I'll share a few examples of some of the coolest experiences I've learned about from clients through the years. I hope they conjure fun and meaningful ideas for you. These run the gamut from low-budget to the highest extremes. Remember, they are not for you to judge but rather to get you thinking about how you might choose to use your resources.

The Road-trippers

One of the best things about retirement is that you have freedom of time, unlike any other period in your life. One couple really went all-in on this concept.

Shortly after they retired, Howard and Ellen packed a few bags, threw them in the back of their SUV, and headed west. "Where are you going? How long will you be gone?" we asked them. They didn't know... It was a modern-day Oregon Trail! They emailed our team along the way and those emails are some of the most impactful notes that I've ever received in my entire career. They were thankful and joyful. This road-tripping duo had plenty of money in their accounts, so they didn't even think about money for gas, hotels, food, and fun. They just went.

And then stopped. And went again at their own pace. Nearly a month later, they returned. That was nearly 15 years ago, and we all still talk about it!

> What about if you don't want to come back home?

Life on the Road

If the freedom of the road is calling you, then perhaps you'll be drawn to RV life like many of our clients. All who've embarked on these journeys have enjoyed them and all have experienced not only amazing adventures but also much work and expenses that belong in the obligation category. Everyone I've known in retirement who's hit and lived on the road has also called it a "chapter," meaning that they enjoy it for a time, and then move on to a more permanent location.

Group Trips

Home rental websites like VRBO® and Airbnb have transformed the idea of traveling with groups. Certainly, a trip with friends can be an incredible experience, but retirees seem to gravitate even more toward the idea of getting their entire family together. Rental properties can be just the way to facilitate these group outings. Some families take regular trips, and some do once-in-a-lifetime experiences. You can create your own adventure *and* price range. My advice is this: Be transparent, intentional, and thoughtful about your budget. If you're planning a family trip, are you going to pay for the lodging? Meals? Flights? Activities? Incidentals? Have the conversations upfront about how expenses will be split up then go have fun!

Turn Left on an Airplane

It's okay to treat yourself—and others—once in a while. One of life's greatest travel experiences is to walk onto an airplane, and turn left… If you don't know what I mean, then you haven't traveled first-class on an international trip. I haven't done this much, but once I got upgraded because the airline over-booked our flight and sent my family home from Europe without me, which forced me to stay an extra day.

While I was lucky to have this experience for free, one of my clients does this regularly for business. They have the goal to create this experience for their parents and fly with them first-class to India.

Whether your ideal travel experiences are for yourself or others, we all know this: Money can't buy you happiness! But, when it comes to travel, flights, transfers, tours, and lodging, it sure can buy you "hassle- free." It might seem crazy to spend your money on perks like these, but remember that these are one-and-done experiences, not obligations that affect your ongoing plan. You can always "not travel" in the future if you can't afford it, and at some point (if you're like all the people we've worked with through the years), there will also be a time in the future when you don't want to travel any longer or you can't.

Obviously, experiences don't have to be all about travel. There are plenty of other exploits to delight in, from concerts to theatre to sports. Some cost a lot, and some don't. Take your time, and find your mix. And remember to bring vacation home with you. I absolutely love the Nespresso machines in many nicer hotel rooms. More than just the coffee and caffeine, I value the feelings and experiences that I associate with so many of these cups. After a busy, fun day of activities on vacation, and while getting ready for dinner or a night out, I've sat for a minute to relax, reflect, and regroup with an espresso. So, I bought a machine for home to experience the same sensations during my "normal" life.

You can plan many big and little experiences in your own world at home. Whether for yourself or others, and whether they happen often or infrequently, my hope for you is that they lead to more "joy" on your balance sheet.

I could go on for pages and pages, regaling you with these fun stories, but it will be way more fun for you to write your own rather than read someone else's! Besides, by now, you might be feeling that what you will do is too focused on you. Maybe you want to think a little more about other people and places in your life. So, let's point our ship in that direction. (There are so many clichés about boats.)

Have you heard these?

BOAT = Bust Out Another Thousand (for all the fuel, insurance, repairs, etc. that go with it).

"The two happiest days in a boat owner's life are the day they buy it and the day they sell it."

"A boat is a hole in the water that you throw your money into."

I offer you this new one, as well: "There is always a bigger boat!"

I use that phrase as a metaphor for life, and I've said for years that it pertains to the comparison of and contentment with anything we might buy or experience in our lives. Consider your dream home, dream boat, or dream trip. Without a doubt, once you purchase one or all of these, you will notice someone else who has it just a little bit better or whose boat/home/car is slightly nicer. It never fails, and these comparisons can drive us crazy!

What the Marina Can Teach You

Never was this comparison more noticeable, profound, or powerful than when I spent a day at the docks in Fort Myers, Florida. Before I take you to the marina, let's go back in time. Prior to COVID, boats were assumed to be one of the worst "assets" to own because, like cars, their value often quickly depreciates. It was in that reality that I was helping clients plan for a new boat. And this wasn't just any old boat… It was an upgrade from a $2,000,000 "dinghy" (his words, not mine) to a 70-foot, $4,200,000 yacht.

Anthony, Angela, and I checked all the right boxes. We projected out their routine expenses and recurring income. We planned for experiences and charitable donations. We made assumptions about the additional financial obligations that would come with operating the boat and created multiple Monte Carlo scenarios to determine retirement success based on selling the boat in the future for a lot or a little. The plan was on track, so Anthony put down a deposit on the boat, and we started to segment money to make the purchase payments while it was being built.

Then, COVID hit! Life stopped, markets dropped, and the plan started to crumble. As Mike Tyson once said, "Everyone has a plan until they get punched in the mouth!" Our carefully crafted boat acquisition plan had been punched in the mouth. During the free fall in the markets, and with major uncertainty about the economy, we re-ran projections. A couple of months later, as production on the boat resumed, Anthony was faced with a decision: Keep making payments during volatile markets and economic turmoil or give up, lose his deposit, and let the dream of a bigger boat sink!

After careful deliberation, Anthony proceeded full steam ahead. Thankfully, four years later, his plan is still afloat (all puns intended), and he and his family and friends have had many incredible experiences on that boat.

Anthony and Angela invited me to visit them on their boat in 2021 when it was docked in Fort Myers, Florida. I took two of my younger boys with me for the tour, and we were blown away by their hospitality, generosity, and the entire experience of sailing and relaxing with them. But the craziest part for me came at the beginning of the trip.

Anthony met us at the marina entrance and walked us down to the pier, where my boys and I gazed at his amazing, beautiful boat with its bright white and deep navy colors glistening in the sun. I'd never seen such an incredible boat up close.

There we were, standing on the pier next to his dream come true, and before escorting us on, he stopped short and pointed left. I turned to see a boat that was even bigger than his. Anthony spent our first minute together telling us about the other boat and how cool it was.

I couldn't make that story up if I wanted to. I knew

Anthony had worked hard for this and was grateful for his new boat, but it was such a perfect, real-world example of my theory that there's always a bigger boat. This reality that there is always a bigger boat (or nicer car, or more luxurious trip) is only made more noticeable because of our social media culture that promotes these great experiences. Getting lost in others' posts can quickly cause us to struggle with comparative envy, and if left unchecked, it can be devastating to a financial plan in retirement. There is another way, however...

Retire Intentionally Exercise

Turn your retirement dreams into commitments! You can start on this to-do anytime you want to; all it takes is a little imagination. I'll help you get started with a form you can fill out based on ideas prior clients have had and what we at IntentGen enjoy. Visit www.retire-intentionally.com. Go ahead, take a moment, and add your own inspiration!

Scan for end of chapter worksheets or visit Retire-Intentionally.com

Chapter 8
Give It Away, Give It Away, Give It Away Now

"Do all the good you can, by all the means you can, in all the ways you can, in all the places you can, at all the times you can, to all the people you can, as long as you ever can."
~John Wesley

Contentment is at the opposite end of the spectrum from comparative envy. Although achieving contentment in our consumeristic culture may seem as far-fetched as achieving enlightenment, I have learned that generosity is a key part of balancing the scales between those two ends of the spectrum. Generosity, in and of itself, is simply about showing kindness to others.

Just as there is always a bigger boat, there is always someone with less. Focusing part of our time and giving money toward people and places who have less creates awareness that we do have enough and that we can be ready to help others.

Living generously in retirement means that we have a readiness to give more of something, like money or time than is strictly necessary or expected. During your accumulation years, it likely felt that there was never enough of either. An intentional retirement can become a time of realizing that you have more than enough of both, so you can have fun figuring out how to impact others with your time and money.

I refer to this as net impact. Your net impact is ultimately what you decide to do with your life and your money when you get past the basics. Remember James and Laurie? They were the couple who decided to make their giving budget at least as big as their golf budget. Let's look at the ways that they, and other people, have started to enjoy giving to people and places that they care about, leading up to and into retirement.

James and Laurie have traditionally given most of their "charitable" money to their church and have scattered other donations between local non-profit organizations that they care about. They have been "cash" givers, which means they gave cash or, more than likely, wrote a check, charged it to a credit card, or set up recurring debits from their checking account to do so.

These are wonderful, intentional methods to give their money to others who need it. It's how James and Laurie were taught to give, and they're the tools they've used as they've grown in their giving to help the people and places that they care about.

Giving from our income/cash flow, by donating cash or writing checks, is likely the foundational way that most people learned to give. It's also likely what allows them to continue to give, and I hope that you've experienced the joy that comes from giving and helping others. But understand, as great as giving cash or writing checks is, these are not the most efficient ways to maximize your intentional giving and net impact.

First, let me expound on what I mean by impact. One definition means to have a strong effect on someone or something. As I stated previously, net impact, in this context, is what you do with your life and your money when you get past the basics. If you want to focus on increasing your net impact in retirement, then there's one key ingredient to add: Intentionality. Be thoughtful, planful, and dream big. While you add intentionality to your financial plan, let's focus on minimizing three financial items: 1) unnecessary fees, 2) risks, and 3) taxes.

Before we go any deeper, let me remind you of the formula for net impact:

Net Worth + Net Income = Net Impact

Broken down, step by step, it works like this: Add up your assets plus all the lifetime income and growth you can expect (easy to do through a Monte Carlo simulation), then subtract your liabilities, routine expenses, and the taxes that you will pay. Everything remaining is your potential to use on experiences for yourself and others and for giving to your family, friends, and places you care about. You can choose to do that accidentally or intentionally.

Once you know your capabilities, you can begin to intentionally plan your net impact during your lifetime, intentionally designate people and places to efficiently receive it at the end of your life, or you can wait and let other people decide what they will do with it upon your death. I refer to this last option as "accidental impact." Likely, in that scenario, the impact is lower, and the taxes and fees are higher.

James and Laurie wanted to impact others more intentionally in their retirement. To start with, we had a lively discussion to clarify the impact they wanted to have and to identify the people and places that would benefit from their generosity. Because it's hard to clearly quantify the ultimate impact their donations would eventually have, we focused on the inputs, meaning where to give and how much. We then began to work through a multi-step process to maximize their efficiency and impact.

These are the topics we discussed and the ways we looked at them through the lens of net impact:

Cash vs. Appreciated Assets

Giving through cash, checks, and credit cards can be viewed the same when it comes to charitable impact: You're giving away money that you've already paid taxes on.

Giving from appreciated assets (investments, real estate, or business interests) is more tax-efficient than giving cash: You'll give away growth that has yet to be taxed. If it's possible in your situation, it's usually more impactful to give appreciated assets.

Standard Deductions vs. Itemized Deductions. If you give away enough cash (or ideally, appreciated assets), you can add it to your mortgage interest, state and local taxes, or medical expenses (plus a few other possibilities), and you may be able to itemize your deductions to further reduce your taxable income. A larger itemized deduction will reduce your current tax liability.

Bunching

If you plan on giving to specific organizations or causes every year, you might consider giving multiple years' gifts all at once, which can give you an even greater itemized deduction. (Please review the limits of this strategy with your accountant because you are fast-forwarding future giving into the current tax year.)

Donor-advised Funds

This tool solves the biggest concern that many people have with bunching their charitable gifts—they don't want to give everything away all at once. If you don't like the idea of giving up control of future gifts, or you're looking for simplicity in tracking your giving, consider a donor-advised fund. This investment account can be opened through community foundations or the charitable arms of most brokerage firms. You will give up the ability to spend the cash or appreciated assets that you've contributed to your fund, but you'll have the potential for a large, itemized deduction in the year you give your money. Furthermore, you get to choose how the funds are invested after you give them, you control the pace at which you grant/give the money from the fund, and you'll determine the places that will ultimately receive the funds when you grant them.

Creative Tools

Qualified Charitable Distributions (QCDs) and Charitable Gift Annuities (CGAs) are two of the most common next-level giving tools.

- QCDs are grants you send from your IRA (assuming you are 70.5-plus) and that you instruct your IRA custodian to send directly to the non-profit you select. The amount distributed isn't counted as part of your potential itemized deduction, but even more beneficially, it isn't counted as part of your income! This benefit means your withdrawal doesn't count toward your Medicare (IRMAA) levels or other tax benefits/penalties based on your adjusted gross income.

- CGAs are tools that allow you to gift appreciated assets to a foundation and receive tax-favorable income for your lifetime. You also have the potential of a tax-deductible gift when you make the donation. Perhaps, more importantly, you might just be giving yourself the gift of living longer. Multiple studies cite actuarial statistics showing people who utilize CGAs tend to live longer than those who don't. I'm not going to extend credibility to this by citing sources because I wonder whether the phenomenon is causation or correlation, but it's an interesting point to ponder.

James and Laurie began to explore and implement these additional ways to give. We set up a donor-advised fund and gifted appreciated shares of stocks and funds. This strategy minimized capital gains taxes they would've owed if they had sold the investments, and it gave them a larger itemized deduction. More importantly, it allowed them to Prioritize and Maximize how much they could give.

Before James retires, they plan on filling up this fund with enough for them to give to places they care about until James reaches age 70.5 and can begin QCDs. This donor-advised fund gives them the freedom to give with confidence, just as other financial strategies give them the freedom to spend with confidence, and that's the greatest advantage.

While I can't tell you yet which tool might fit best in your situation or whether what you choose might help you live longer, I could provide countless examples that illustrate the benefits of living generously.

We all know that when we give, it helps others.

What these case studies also illustrate (and there are plenty of scientific studies to back this up) is that giving does amazing things *to* us, as well as *through* us.

I have uncovered a truth that I've seen play out in my life and that of others, and this truth is that God wants generosity FOR us, not just FROM us. Whether you approach your giving from a spiritual or practical perspective or both, I believe that it will unlock incredible potential for you to explore the impact that you hope to have during your life.

Marc and Maryjo, who I profiled earlier, wanted to do all that charitable giving and more. They wanted to focus their impact on their family as well as non-profits. They have been the recipients of lifetime gifts from their parents and are eager to help their adult

children get started on a strong financial footing.
As part of this, they've had conversations that have
helped them learn about saving, giving, and investing.
Additionally, they chose to give some money during
their lifetimes to help their kids buy homes.

Remember that tax question I asked earlier about
if tax rates will be higher or lower? If you recall, we
can't answer that question precisely because we don't
know the future. But we do know the present, and
that current tax rate consideration is only the first
question we need to address. The second question
is bigger and perhaps even more important: Do you
think the tax rate of the people or places who get
your money will be higher or lower than yours now
and later? Here's what to consider:

Are your beneficiaries (children, nieces/
nephews, siblings) successful?

Are they making more money than you ever
made, or at least more than what you're making
now?

Are they going to receive an inheritance from
someone else?

If you don't know their income and tax rate, either
ask them or make a guess, and then check the tax
charts. Taking that information into account, ask
yourself if the most efficient lifetime tax plan is to
defer your IRA and leave it to them.

If their income and future tax bracket is likely lower than yours, then it might be. But if their income and tax brackets are likely higher than yours, and they have to pay taxes on everything from your IRA at their rate, then tax deferral on your IRA is likely not the most efficient way to increase your net impact. There are other strategies that should be explored.

What about your church that you support so faithfully? Or the local food pantry where you've loyally given and volunteered throughout your lifetime? Will they miss you and your money when you're gone?

What if you left some IRA money to your favorite charity? What's their tax rate? If you don't know, you don't need to ask or guess; I'll just tell you. The tax rate for a 501(c)(3) is 0%. That's right… if you leave your tax- deferred IRA to your favorite charitable organization, there are no income taxes due, and the organization gets everything. That's great for the non-profit organization, but what about your kids and grandkids? We'll come back to the charitable part in a little bit, but let's return to Marc's and Maryjo's story.

Marc and Maryjo had been helping their kids already, but like James' and Laurie's charitable giving, they'd been doing small gifts as "cash." If they were going to give larger cash gifts to their three children, up to the $18,000 annual exclusion amount for gift taxes, *it would take more creativity because they didn't have the cash. They had been thinking about this dilemma and came up with three options on their own:*

1. Withdraw from their IRAs and pay ordinary income taxes at their 24% bracket, potentially driving them up into the 32% bracket while also causing them to pay more for their Medicare premiums (for IRMAA penalties).

2. Sell investments and then withdraw from their taxable portfolio and pay capital gains taxes at the federal rate of 15% or 20%, plus a state rate of 5% and a 3.8% Medicare tax on capital gains (net investment income tax), with the potential of this income causing them to pay more for their Medicare premiums (IRMAA).

3. Withdraw from their ROTH IRAs and pay no taxes; This seemed most ideal for them in the moment, but it means they are missing out on their lifetime of tax-free growth on that money.

What Marc and Maryjo didn't initially consider was their ability to give appreciated stocks and funds from their taxable portfolios directly to their kids. As it turned out, this was one of the most effective ways for them to maximize their impact because it minimized their family's taxes.

Of course, your situation may be different, and you should consult a tax advisor, but it provided several benefits for them:

- *Their kids wouldn't have to pay the 3.8% Medicare tax (because their income was below the threshold).*

- *The state income tax on capital gains wouldn't apply (because the kids live in one of eight states that don't tax capital gains).*

- *The additional income had no impact on the kids' Medicare premiums (IRMAA) because the children are young adults and don't have Medicare.*

Marc and Maryjo hoped to each give $18,000 to each of their three children (and their spouses) when the kids were ready to purchase a home. So, in this scenario, with an eventual total of 12 gifts of $18,000, the tax savings from this strategy could be in the tens of thousands—all by gifting appreciated assets rather than selling and gifting cash.

These lifetime gifts are just the beginning for many people exploring their intentional impact. Estate gifts to children, grandchildren, and charities are usually the biggest components of this impact.

KISS (keep it simple, smarty!)

Ward and June have been great stewards of their finances throughout their lifetime. Their careers in social work and education never resulted in huge incomes or stock performance plans, but they raised their children in the Chicago suburbs, spent carefully, gave generously, invested consistently, and watched their net worth grow. As they prepared for retirement and transitioned from accumulation to distribution, they also focused on net income, and we implemented strategies to help them create recurring income to cover their lifestyle.

Their plan was strong, and our projections gave them the confidence to move into a newer, larger home that was closer to their children and grandchildren. The plan unexpectedly became even stronger when they inherited money from their families. During a review, we re-ran their projections through a Monte Carlo analysis and overlayed their net worth on the tax-efficiency checklist.

Ward admitted that he doesn't enjoy talking about finances and doesn't consider himself a numbers guy. But, as we talked about what they wanted to do with the potential of surplus money that they might not need, he moved the TEC to the middle of my desk and turned it for all of us to see. He then said one of the best lines that simplifies the complexity of this whole process: "It looks like we just need to move some money from here to here, and from here to here," as he pointed to the columns on the TEC.

That was precisely it!

Now, I just needed to ask a few questions and do a good job listening. We didn't have to be complex in the moment; I only had to help them specify the percentages that they wanted to direct toward their family and church and charities. We meet regularly to review the annual process of transitioning that money to align with their purpose.

That process will begin to accelerate this year as Ward reaches the age of RMDs, which for him is 73. Ward and June will continue to give via qualified charitable distributions (QCDs), taking money directly out of the middle column and giving it to organizations they care about. And they'll give some of the extra RMDs to kids and re-save some of it into life insurance that will pay tax-free to their children and grandchildren at their deaths. Based on how high their income gets as they pay for experiences they value and appreciate, we'll determine if there's additional money in their tax and IRMAA brackets to shift into ROTH IRAs or taxable accounts to line up with their near-term and long-term spending, saving, and giving plans.

This thoughtful couple is telling us how to prioritize the balance between the columns, and we are handling the details so they can go back to grandkids, gardening, and the other activities that keep them young.

Retire Intentionally Exercise

I've made understanding the differences between the various types of deductions, bunching, and donor-advised funds easier to envision and apply to your life's circumstances.

Please visit www.retire-intentionally.com for your free tools.

Scan for end of chapter worksheets or visit Retire-Intentionally.com

Chapter 9
To Be(queath) or Not to Be(queath)

"An inheritance is something you leave for someone. A legacy is something you leave in someone."
~Reggie Joiner

Net impact is about much more than money—it includes our time, knowledge, and experiences and how we invest all those qualities into the people and places we care about.

For the purposes of this book, I'm focusing on the financial aspects of your impact because most people in the US and around the world worry more about running out of money than about running out of time. Said differently, most people worry about outliving their money. In one of my interviews, my client Jack shared the opposite concern, and it has shaped my thinking as I've worked on this book.

Little Ditty about Jack and Allison

Jack and his wife, Allison, are businesspeople who are engaged with many community organizations. They are educated and experienced investors who've worked with several financial planning companies through the years, including my own. They invest in real estate, stocks, index funds, and retirement plans. They have

*prepared well and look at retirement as a beginning—
they're excited to build a new home, travel more, and
become even more involved with non-profits.*

*Perhaps you are fortunate enough to be on a similar
track as Allison and Jack. You have a high recurring
income relative to your routine expenses, which
gives you a high probability score on Monte Carlo
projections. You have diversified your assets across
investment classes, tax strategies, and timeframes.
You have been a great steward of your resources, and
you're lucky enough not to worry about running out
of money.*

The simple outline of your financial plan
looks like this:

Net worth: Check!
Net income: Check!

Net impact is the third piece. Now, it's time to
really dig into it! If you have already determined that
there will be an element of your financial plan left
for someone else, then it's time to start thinking big.
Although net impact conversations are beneficial for
everyone, the possibilities to create lasting impact are
nearly endless if you can expand your thinking when
you're in this position of financial strength. Rather
than relaxing and thinking *I've made it*, perhaps it is
time to begin questioning *what else can be done*?

Changing your perspective can help you transition from an attitude of scarcity to a mindset of abundant thinking. Many thought leaders in the financial world have written about attitudes of scarcity and abundance.

Scarcity leads people to worry about running out of money and causes them to avoid doing what they'd like to do. Abundance leads us to a mindset that there is enough, and we can do more with what we have.

Stanley Hewitt, the former CEO of Fortune 500 company Thrivent Financial, adds another perspective beyond abundance. He refers to a mindset of generosity that allows us to focus our abundance on others, not just ourselves.

Imagine a plan so strong that you don't have to worry about basic living expenses, one so flexible that you can jump at opportunities for cool experiences, and a mindset to help others along the way and at the end!

So, if you have the resources, what's stopping you from living this way? It's often one of two issues:

1. What if?
2. Net worth!

"What if" can be a disease. It can cause analysis paralysis, lead to inaction, and even make people just plain "grumpy." Early symptoms often show up with worrisome questions, like:

What if I live a really long time? What if I need extended healthcare?

What if my kids or grandkids need help with life circumstances?

What if the market crashes? What if inflation spikes again?

These are all legitimate questions and concerns, but take heart and know that proper planning can minimize unnecessary risks. There are tools designed for mitigating each of your risks, and your Monte Carlo simulations can project the negative impact of these financial risks. But remember, maximizing your net impact only means *minimizing* unnecessary risks, fees, and taxes. It doesn't mean eliminating every risk possible.

Perhaps you've been counseled to hope for the best and plan for the worst. Well, that sounds somewhat miserable... Risks are a reality we must live with. I prefer to plan for the best and have contingencies to hedge some of the risks that concern me.

As an example, I plan to live a long time, so I work at staying healthy and active. My wife and I use financial instruments like market-based investments, insurance policies, real estate, and annuities to provide growth opportunities, tax deferral, and prepare for income and tax efficiency during a long retirement. We also save significant amounts of our income now to prepare for a future that we hope is filled with travel and experiences with our friends, our four children, and hopefully future grandchildren. Of course, there are things that can derail that plan, so I hedge those risks.

One way we do that is by balancing "living life now" with "saving for later." Because our retirement plan's probability score gives us confidence that we're on track for retirement, we give ourselves permission to spend more now on travel or experiences rather than feeling like we have to save everything to be ready for later. If you're not yet retired, a thoughtful plan and projection can give you that same confidence so you can "enjoy it now" rather than waiting for later.

Of course, there are too many examples to remind us that none of us have later guaranteed. To help hedge that risk of not getting to "later on," I have disability income insurance to replace income in case I become sick or get hurt and can't work. I also have life insurance to provide funds, pay off debt, and replace income if I die too soon.

If you're in retirement already, and you've prepared well, then your hopes, dreams, and risks are different than mine. From a position of strength, you can create a budget to travel internationally until you're 90; rent a home in Florida every year so you can play pickleball in the winter until you're 100; spend your money on golf so you can shoot your age when you're 85; and accumulate college funds not just for your grandchildren, but also for your great-grandchildren!

Dream, commit, and create habits to help you reach those goals, and then go do it. Don't let risks hold you back from using your money when you can.

But "what ifs" still often plague people and limit their plans. If you're that worried about the what if of extended healthcare, then plan to be healthy, eat well, and stay active. Set aside funds specifically for healthcare or purchase long-term care insurance to hedge that risk. I know insurance might be a waste of money, but paying premiums to hedge the big risk of significant expenses could give you the confidence to start spending money now rather than saving it for "what ifs" down the road. In the movie The Shawshank Redemption, Andy Dufresne said, "I guess it comes down to a simple choice really. Get busy living or get busy dying." That reminder is especially relevant to your intentional retirement.

There is another relevant phrase that I've heard for years to describe retirement phases: The go-go years, the slow-go years, and the no-go years.

If you segment a potential 30-year retirement across these phases, it could be that you have 10 years within each period. If you're really healthy and lucky, maybe you'll have 15 go-go years, 10 slow-go, and 5 no-go years before you're gone. So, why not have fun spending, giving, and living during the go-go years rather than worrying about the what-ifs, even if it means you have less to spend in the slow-go and no-go years?

What ifs paralyze us from living full lives. My friends, Jack and Allison, who think they are more likely to run out of time before they run out of money, are busy living. Theirs is a life that is and will be filled with net impact throughout all the years they have.

Warren Buffett's Pledge

The second big concern that holds people back from increasing their net impact is that silly little number that keeps popping back into our conscience... net worth! Why do we care so much about net worth? If your goal is to leave a lot behind, then I guess I can understand. Yet most people I've interviewed and worked with do not put "huge inheritance for kids" at the top of their list.

We all know the name Warren Buffett. I think most of us would agree he's one of the best investors ever and that we could probably learn a lot from him on that particular topic. I also think he's one of the most generous people, and not just because of how much he has given or will give. What inspires me most is not the amount of money but the percentage that he has committed to giving during his lifetime. Here is an excerpt from Warren Buffett's Giving Pledge:

"More than 99% of my wealth will go to philanthropy during my lifetime or at my death. Measured by dollars, this commitment is large. In a comparative sense, though, many individuals give more to others every day. Millions of people who regularly contribute to churches, schools, and other organizations thereby relinquish the use of funds that would otherwise benefit their own families. The dollars these people drop into a collection plate or give to the United Way mean forgone movies, dinners out, or other personal pleasures. In contrast, my family and I will give up nothing we need or want by fulfilling this 99% pledge."

As much as I love Warren Buffett's pledge and his subsequent challenges to other wealthy individuals, it's hard for most of us to grasp the concept of what he's talking about because our numbers are not in the billions. You may want to donate to worthy causes, create fun experiences for yourself and others, and give money to your family when you pass. But trying to do all that can put a strain on your net worth number. In fact, it could cause it to go down a lot…

But if you're focused on net impact, so what?! Julie found a counterbalance to that net worth focus when she added "JOY" to her balance sheet. When Julie updates her net worth statement, she can reflect on her experiences even if her net worth isn't always growing.

I found a counterbalance to my scarcity mindset when I added "generosity" to our balance sheet. Now, when I update our personal net worth statement at the end of each year, I literally track the cumulative lifetime total for the money that my wife and I have invested in places we care about. It's one way to measure our inputs toward a long-term net impact that we might never see. It's also a way for me to balance contentment and aspiration. Because of our giving, our net worth may never grow to as much as it could have. And I couldn't be happier.

So, what else needs to be tracked on your net worth statement? And what might need to be taken off it so you can focus better on the impact, inheritance, and legacy you want to leave? Warren Buffett also once said that when it comes to inheritances, "Leave the children enough so they can do anything but not enough that they can do nothing."

Could you, or should you, add to your net income to help you align your money with your priorities, values, joy, and generosity? Could you, or should you, intentionally cause your net worth to decrease in order to create more impact along the way and leave a more intentional legacy with the people and places you care about?

These questions are not meant to be answered quickly or taken lightly. My hope is that they encourage you to think and help you move past the two biggest limitations that might hold back your net impact, those nagging worries about "what if" and "how much."

Make the Magic Happen!

Our time together is coming to a close, and it's only fitting that we wrap up by going back to my Disney World story at the beginning of this book. But first, a few reminders and takeaways…

Regardless of your net worth, net income, or your Monte Carlo probability score, I want to remind you that you are a champion of retirement planning. If you are fortunate enough to even think about retirement, you have more income and assets than most people in this world. If you can think about retirement in terms of purpose and impact, you are in an even smaller group of people.

According to a recent survey by Northwestern Mutual[6] and an article in Kiplinger in April 2024[7], the majority of retirees surveyed believe that they will need nearly $1,500,000 to retire. Fidelity's annual studies point to guidelines that suggest you should have 6 times your salary by age 50, 8 times by 60, and 10 times by age 67.[8]

As I have emphasized throughout this book, I advise you to focus much less on those numbers and, instead, concentrate much more on what you need to activate your income and impact.

If you're already confident in your plan, then I hope this book has helped you expand your thinking about your net impact. We at IntentGen would be honored to help you maximize it.

---

[6] "Americans Believe They Will Need $1.46 Million to Retire Comfortably According to Northwestern Mutual 2024 Planning & Progress Study." Newsroom | Northwestern Mutual. Accessed August 1, 2024. https://news.northwesternmutual.com/2024-04-02-Americans-Believe- They-Will-Need-1-46-Million-to-Retire-Comfortably-According-to- Northwestern-Mutual-2024-Planning-Progress-Study.

[7] Kelsey M. Simasko, Esq. "How Women Can Win the Retirement Savings Struggle." Kiplinger.com, August 1, 2024. https://www.kiplinger.com/retirement/how-women-can-win-the- retirement-savings-struggle.

[8] Viewpoints, Fidelity. "Top 3 Questions about Saving for Retirement." Fidelity, March 6, 2024. https://www.fidelity.com/learning- center/personal-finance/questions-on-saving-for-retirement.

If you haven't yet achieved confidence around your retirement income and impact, then I encourage you to refocus your financial commitments and recreate habits. You can live more like the millionaire next door and become a prodigious accumulator of wealth. Spend less, save a higher percentage of your income, pay off debt, give more, and diversify your tax-efficiency checklist. You can get there, and we can help.

Regardless of your status, I hope you noticed throughout this book that most of the stories I shared didn't have net worth numbers attached...and that was on purpose. The amount you need for retirement will vary dramatically from person to person, based on your basic living expenses, recurring income, and your desire for impact.

Our company actively engages with people who are retiring intentionally and who have net worth numbers from $300,000 to $30,000,000. Remember, it's not your net worth that will determine your retirement; it's your income relative to your expenses, the experiences that you value, and how you perceive your purpose and impact.

Your Why Determines Your What

Author, speaker, and thought-leader Simon Sinek gave an incredible TED Talk entitled "Start with Why!" I'd encourage you to listen and ponder his comments. The core message is that when selling products and solving problems (and, I would add, planning your retirement), it is imperative that we start with "why" rather than "how" or "what."

Recall that David, the owner of the Swiss chalet, talked about this "why" perspective, as well. If you're taking on more (or less) risk with your investments, why are you doing it? If you're minimizing taxes or downsizing your home, why are you doing it? Start with why, then act like a two-year-old, and ask yourself… *why, why, why*?

Why are you retiring in the first place? Why do you want to stop working?

- Why are you spending so much or so little?
- Why are you worried about maintaining or growing your net worth?
- Why do you want to leave money or assets to your kids?
- Why do you give to other places?

Why did my wife and I choose all those years ago to take our four young kids to Disney? We did it for a variety of reasons:

- We value family time and new experiences.
- We wanted to see our boys smile and laugh.

- We hoped it would bring us all closer together. We had heard it was a magical place.

What we didn't hear about Disney was everything else accompanying the magic: The irregular schedules, the cost, the unexpected sicknesses, and all the other details that didn't go according to plan. But that's no reason not to go. In fact, I'd recommend Disney to anyone.

In the same way, retirement will be filled with all of the above, both good and bad. But, if you are ready to live an intentional retirement that focuses on purpose and net impact, I'd recommend it to anyone. We can help you better understand your net income and net worth and get you focused on starting with why so you can increase your net impact! Although there are some aspects we can't control, like time…

I Couldn't Have Said It Better

During a recent meeting with Charlie and June, who are clients in their late 80s, my team and I finished reviewing all the details of their plan. The projections were strong, the asset allocation and location were balanced, the net income was more than sufficient, and their net worth was higher than ever. Charlie and June were content and focused on enjoying life.

But just before we signed off Zoom, Charlie stopped me and said there's one more thing. Then, he surprised me with this request: "I'd like to trade my money for time!" He said it with a smile, but I could see a sad look in his eyes... It was bittersweet.

There's not a lot that Charlie can do about time now, but you and I can learn from him. Whether you're at the beginning of your retirement years or nearing the end, you still have money and time. Use them intentionally!

Your Final Retire Intentionally Exercise

Continue your Intentional Retirement journey now by answering these two questions:

1. What will your first action be?

2. Who are you appointing as your accountability partner? You might consider IntentGen Financial Partners, a spouse, friend, relative, or other advisor.

This information, taking action, and forming accountability partners will get you well on your way to creating more net impact and living your Intentional Retirement.

Scan for end of chapter worksheets or visit Retire-Intentionally.com

.

Acknowledgments

To Kristin, my love and life partner. Thank you for encouraging me to write "real." Without our conversations and your corrections on my writing and speaking through the years, this book would have been twice as long and half as good.

To Corey, my friend and business partner. Thanks for encouraging me to find the words for our company, even when you're often the one with the idea or action. This book wouldn't have happened without your trust and confidence. Even though the words on these pages are mine, we've shared the stories together along the way, and our impact is forever intertwined.

To my parents, Keith Larson and Ginger Anderson-Larson, and my in-laws, Mark and Rita Bawden. Thanks for teaching and modeling compassion, creativity, and commitments to generosity. The way that you care for your families and your communities is an inspiration.

To Hilary, my editor, book partner, and person I've never met (except on Zoom). Thanks for encouraging and guiding me. You believed in me from the start and made this project come to life. Although an author gets their name on the book, I've learned it takes an incredible team to make a book, and you led the way for my team.

About the Author

Zac Larson has dedicated over two decades to improving his clients' lives and growing a company that positively impacts the community. Guided by a philosophy centered on purpose and service, Zac chose a path divergent from conventional norms, prioritizing thoughtful, client-focused financial partnerships.

His career began with Thrivent Financial, where Zac and his business partner, Corey Schmidt, found a platform to align their professional pursuits and personal values. Zac and Corey co-founded IntentGen Financial Partners in 2018 with the goal of delivering more value to their clients, team, and community. Their specialized brand of financial planning, asset management, and community engagement enables them to live out their mission of *empowering people to live intentionally.*

Zac's current roles focus on enhancing IntentGen's culture and brand while also building client and community relationships. His client-facing expertise supports the company's process to help strategize and maximize plans for retirement income, investment management, wealth transfer, tax efficiency, and charitable giving. His leadership goals are to create opportunities for employees, clients, and the community to live intentionally, grow purposefully, and experience the joy of living generously.

Beyond his professional endeavors, Zac finds fulfillment in his role as a husband to Kristin, whom he married in 2003, and as a father to their four teenage sons. He actively engages in his community, serving on non-profit boards and coaching his sons' basketball teams. Zac recharges by golfing, scuba diving, skiing, cycling, and traveling. Through his multifaceted pursuits, Zac is committed to fostering a legacy of intentional and generous living that he strives to pay forward every day.

Disclaimers and Definitions

Investment advisory services offered through Thrivent Advisor Network, LLC., a registered investment adviser and a subsidiary of Thrivent. Advisory Persons of Thrivent provide advisory services under a "doing business as" name or may have their own legal business entities. However, advisory services are engaged exclusively through Thrivent Advisor Network, LLC, a registered investment adviser. IntentGen Financial Partners and Thrivent Advisor Network, LLC are not affiliated companies. Information in this message is for the intended recipient[s] only. Please visit our website www.intentgen.com for important disclosures.

Securities offered through Thrivent Investment Management Inc. ("TIMI"), member FINRA and SIPC, and a subsidiary of Thrivent, the marketing name for Thrivent Financial for Lutherans. Thrivent.com/disclosures. TIMI and IntentGen Financial Partners are not affiliated companies.

Clients are under no obligation to purchase additional products and services from Advisory Persons and all advisory services are described in the advisory agreement with Thrivent Advisor Network, LLC.

This material is provided for informational purposes only and is not solely intended to be relied upon as a forecast, research or investment advice, and is not a recommendation, offer or solicitation to buy or sell any securities or to adopt any investment strategy. The views and strategies described may not be suitable for all investors. They also do not include all fees or expenses that may be incurred by investing in specific products. Past performance is no guarantee of future results. Investments will fluctuate and when redeemed may be worth more or less than when originally invested. You cannot invest directly in an index. The opinions expressed are subject to change as subsequent conditions vary. Advisory services offered through Thrivent Advisor Network, LLC.

The material presented includes information and opinions provided by a party not related to Thrivent Advisor Network. It has been obtained from sources deemed reliable; but no independent verification has been made, nor is its accuracy or completeness guaranteed. The opinions expressed may not necessarily represent those of Thrivent Advisor Network or its affiliates. They are provided solely for information purposes and are not to be construed as solicitations or offers to buy or sell any products, securities, or services. They also do not include all fees or expenses that may be incurred by investing in specific products. Past performance is no guarantee of future results. Investments will fluctuate and when redeemed may be worth more or less than when originally invested. You cannot invest directly in an index. The opinions expressed are subject to change as subsequent conditions vary. Thrivent Advisor Network and its affiliates accept no liability for loss or damage of any kind arising from the use of this information.

IMPORTANT: Advisory Person(s) may use proprietary financial planning tools, calculators and third-party tools and materials ("Third-Party Materials") to develop your financial planning recommendations. The projections or other information generated by Third-Party Materials regarding the likelihood of various investment outcomes are hypothetical in nature, do not reflect actual investment results, and are not guarantees of future results. Results may vary with each use and over time. Thrivent Advisor Network, LLC and its advisors do not provide legal, accounting or tax advice. Consult your attorney and or tax professional regarding these situations.

The return assumptions in Third-Party Materials are not reflective of any specific product, and do not include any fees or expenses that may be incurred by investing in specific products. The actual returns of a specific product may be more or less than the returns used. It is not possible to directly invest in an index. Financial forecasts, rates of return, risk, inflation, and other assumptions may be used as the basis for illustrations. They should not be considered a guarantee of future performance or a guarantee of achieving overall financial objectives. Past performance is not a guarantee or a predictor of future results of either the indices or any particular investment. Investing involves risks, including the possible loss of principal.

Investment advisory services are offered through Thrivent Advisor Network, LLC, a registered investment adviser. This material, in and of itself, does not create an investment advisory relationship subject to the Investment Advisers Act of 1940.

The purpose of the book is to illustrate how accepted financial and estate planning principles may improve your current situation. The term "plan" or "planning," when used within this book, does not imply that a recommendation has been made to implement one or more financial plans or make a particular investment. You should use this book to help you focus on the factors that are most important to you. Review the Financial Planning Disclosure Document and the Financial Planning Agreement for a full description of the services offered and fees.

Investment advisory services offered through Thrivent Advisor Network, LLC., (herein referred to as "Thrivent"), a registered investment adviser. Clients will separately engage an unaffiliated broker-dealer or custodian to safeguard their investment advisory assets. Review the Thrivent Advisor Network Client Relationship Summary, Financial Planning and Consulting Services, Investment Management Services (Non-Wrap) and Wrap-Fee Program brochures for a full description of services, fees and expenses, available at Thriventadvisornetwork.com. Thrivent Advisor Network, LLC's Advisory Persons may also be registered representatives of a broker-dealer to offer securities products.

Certain Thrivent Advisor Network LLC advisors may also be registered representatives of a broker-dealer to offer securities products. Advisory Persons of Thrivent provide advisory services under a "doing business as" name or may have their own legal business entities. However, advisory services are engaged exclusively through Thrivent Advisor Network, LLC, a registered investment adviser. Please visit our website www. thriventadvisornetwork.com for important disclosures.

Any specific securities identified and described do not represent all of the securities purchased, sold, or recommended for advisory clients. The reader should not assume that investments in the securities identified and discussed were or will be profitable. A summary description of the principal risks of investing in a particular model is available upon request. There can be no assurance that a model will achieve its investment objectives. Investment strategies employed by the advisor in selecting investments for the model portfolio may not result in an increase in the value of your investment or in overall performance equal to other investments. The model portfolio's investment objectives may be changed at any time without prior notice. Portfolio allocations are based on a model portfolio, which may not be suitable for all investors. Clients should also consider the transactions costs and/or tax consequences that might result from rebalancing a model portfolio. Frequent rebalancing may incur additional costs and/or tax consequences versus less rebalancing. Please notify us if there have been any changes to your financial situation or your investment objectives, or if you would like to place or modify any reasonable restrictions on the management of your account.

This communication may include forward looking statements. Specific forward-looking statements can be identified by the fact that they do not relate strictly to historical or current facts and include, without limitation, words such as "may," "will," "expects," "believes," "anticipates," "plans," "estimates," "projects," "targets," "forecasts," "seeks," "could'" or the negative of such terms or other variations on such terms or comparable terminology.

Definitions:

A 401(k) is a tax-advantaged retirement savings plan. Named after a section of the U.S. Internal Revenue Code, the 401(k) is an employer-provided, defined-contribution plan. The employer may match employee contributions; with some plans, the match is mandatory.

A 403(b) plan (also called a tax-sheltered annuity or TSA plan) is a retirement plan offered by public schools and certain 501(c)(3) tax-exempt organizations. Employees save for retirement by contributing to individual accounts. Employers can also contribute to employees' accounts.

A 501(c)(3) organization is a United States corporation, trust, unincorporated association or other type of organization exempt from federal income tax under section 501(c)(3) of Title 26 of the United States Code.

A 529 plan is a tax-advantaged savings plan designed to encourage saving for future education costs. 529 plans, legally known as "qualified tuition plans," are sponsored by states, state agencies, or educational institutions and are authorized by Section 529 of the Internal Revenue Code.

Adjusted gross income, also known as (AGI), is defined as total income minus deductions, or "adjustments" to income that you are eligible to take.

A certificate of deposit (CD) is a type of savings account that pays a fixed interest rate on money held for an agreed-upon period of time. CD rates are usually higher than savings accounts, but you lose withdrawal flexibility. If you withdraw your CD funds early, you'll be charged a penalty.

COVID (COrona VIrus Disease) is the new name of this disease is coronavirus disease 2019, abbreviated as COVID-19. In COVID-19, 'CO' stands for 'corona,' 'VI' for 'virus,' and 'D' for the disease. Formerly, this disease was referred to as "2019 novel coronavirus" or "2019-nCoV."

Full retirement age (FRA) is the age at which you can receive full retirement benefits from Social Security. It's also known as normal retirement age. Full retirement age varies depending on the year you were born. FRA is 66 years and two months for people born in 1955, and it gradually rises to 67 for those born in 1960 or later.

An individual retirement account (IRA) is a long-term, tax-advantaged savings account that individuals with earned income can use to save for the future.

A Monte Carlo simulation is a way to model the probability of different outcomes in a process that cannot easily be predicted due to the intervention of random variables. It is a technique used to understand the impact of risk and uncertainty. A Monte Carlo simulation requires assigning multiple values to an uncertain variable to achieve multiple results and then averaging the results to obtain an estimate. These simulations assume perfectly efficient markets.

A Prodigious Accumulator of Wealth (PAW) is a name coined by the authors of The Millionaire Next Door. It is the reciprocal of the more common UAW, accumulating usually well over one tenth of the product of the individual's age and their realized pretax income.

Required minimum distributions (RMDs) are the minimum amounts you must withdraw from your retirement accounts each year. You generally must start taking withdrawals from your traditional IRA, SEP IRA, SIMPLE IRA, and retirement plan accounts when you reach age 72 (73 if you reach age 72 after Dec. 31, 2022).

A Roth 401(k) is an employer-sponsored retirement savings account that is funded using after-tax dollars. This means that income tax is paid immediately on the earnings that the employee deducts from each paycheck and deposits into the account. As long as certain conditions are met—that is, you must be at least 59 ½, and you must have had the account for at least five years—withdrawals from the account are tax-free upon retirement.

A Roth IRA is an Individual Retirement Account to which you contribute after-tax dollars. While there are no current-year tax benefits, your contributions and earnings can grow tax-free, and you can withdraw them tax-free and penalty free after age 59½ and once the account has been open for five years.

Under Accumulator of Wealth (UAW) is a name coined by the authors of The Millionaire Next Door used to represent individuals who have a low net wealth compared to their income.

Made in the USA
Columbia, SC
05 November 2024

45441334R00107